The Life and Wisdom of Gwen Frostic

by

Sheryl James

Library of Congress Cataloging-in-Publication Data

James, Sheryl.
The life and wisdom of Gwen Frostic / by Sheryl James.
p.   cm.
ISBN 1-886947-85-6
1. Frostic, Gwen. 2. Physically handicapped artists—United
States Biography. 3. Poets, American—20th century
Biography. 4. Women printers—United States Biography.
5. Linoleum block-printing, American. I. Title
NX512.F76J36   1999
811′.54—dc21
[B]   99-33315
CIP

All inquiries should be addressed to:

Sleeping Bear Press
121 South Main
P.O. Box 20
Chelsea, MI 48118

www.sleepingbearpress.com

Printed in the United States

10 9 8 7 6 5 4 3 2 1

Foreword

There lives in our great North country an extraordinary woman who makes pictures that celebrate Michigan. She has made these pictures for nearly 50 years now by herself. Using hands crippled by age and stiffened by a childhood disease, she carefully carves linoleum blocks for hours until, all of a sudden an image appears: a chickadee, a White Pine, Queen Anne's Lace. Sometimes the images are more generous: a field of Michigan wildflowers, a sky cluttered with Michigan butterflies, a Great Lakes shoreline.

These linoleum block images are stamped onto stationery products made at her self-designed shop, Presscraft Papers in Benzonia, a magical place of huge boulders, real bark wall coverings and a natural flowing well. Her pictures also illustrate books of her unusual prose, which looks like poetry and provokes new thoughts about Michigan nature—and human nature too.

If you have lived in Michigan any length of time, you already know the woman is Gwen Frostic. You have likely bought her products, seen them on a friend's coffee table, perhaps received a letter with the telltale forest creatures only Gwen can immortalize.

Gwen Frostic, 93, is a Michigan institution, a designation few people can claim, and she may be Michigan's most unusual natural resource. Like the Petoskey stone or Michigan's mitten shape, she is unique, a human being that has lived her life her way without regrets. It is a life worth studying.

There are traditional reasons to appreciate Gwen Frostic: she has, in a sense, helped preserve Michigan nature through her art. She became a millionaire back in the 1960s, a rare accomplishment for middle-aged, single women at that time—or any. She has, through her longevity, witnessed most of Michigan's 20th century, participated in some of its key events, and watched how this century has changed her beloved state. She has seen Michigan grow up.

Gwen has written several books which include her art and her prose. Gwen's second book was titled *A Walk With Me*. A walk through Gwen Frostic's life is a walk through Michigan history.

Born in 1906, Gwen remembers seeing her uncle off to World War I at the ornate Ann Arbor train station now known as a restaurant, the Gandy Dancer. She remembers her mother's suffrage activities, her family's horse and buggy and not having to go to school November 11, 1918.

She recalls the first radios. "The first one we had was just a tube and a box wound with wire," she said in 1998. "You hooked it up to the telephone. If the telephone rang, you had to disconnect the radio."

Gwen played on Grosse Ile when it was still open spaces. She remembers streetcars in Detroit and attended Western Michigan University when it consisted mainly of three, 1905 buildings. She made copper vases for Mrs. Henry Ford and worked at the Willow Run bomber plant during World War II.

She has lived in Michigan's thumb, down river in Wyandotte and, since 1955, in the Frankfort/Benzonia area. The only foreign country she has visited is Canada back in '55. Other than a few business trips, she has been right here in Michigan for 93 years.

For all of the above reasons, Gwen has received dozens of awards, honorary degrees and other recognition, such as the day named in her honor by Governor Bill Milliken and induction into the Michigan Women's Hall of Fame.

But Gwen Frostic is particularly inspiring for the way she has challenged the meaning of the word "handicapped." A childhood illness left Gwen with visible physical aftereffects. She never considered herself handicapped but most others did. Gwen grew up knowing that, facing the assumption by some that "handicapped" people were by definition less intelligent, less capable, less desirable. At the same time she accomplished things few people do against heavy odds, setting up a strange, double edged existence: Gwen Frostic has always been handicapped, she has never been handicapped.

"People ask me what her handicap is," says Gwen's sister, Helen Warren of Dearborn. "And I say, 'You tell me.'"

Add to all of this Gwen's unforgettable personality. Few who meet her forget her. Shrewd, smart and entertaining, Gwen can hold her own with anyone and is known for her apt one-liners such as: "Everybody thinks they're more important than they are," or "Just because a person is older doesn't mean they don't have new ideas."

A biography seems only fitting at this point in time. Gwen Frostic doesn't really agree. Her reluctance stems partly from her sense of privacy, partly from her basic belief that to analyze anything too closely is to destroy it. She does not think she has done anything special. Besides, hard-headed and stubborn, Gwen Frostic never looks back. Why, she asks, should anyone else? This, and her naturally blunt manner resulted in interviews—initially done for a 1999 *Detroit Free Press* article—that were at times less than loquacious:

"You once told a friend the first million was the hardest. Would it be accurate to call you a millionaire, a multi-millionaire?"

"I wouldn't call myself anything."

"What peaks and valleys have you had in your life, the major ups and downs?"

"There haven't been any peaks and valleys."

As a result of Gwen's reluctance, much of what appears in this biography comes from sources other than her—from friends, fans, family, observers, historical records and newspaper archives. The woman that emerges is neither handicapped nor unaffected by illness, neither saint nor sinner. She is not the sweet old lady so many assume she is once they notice her so-called handicap. She has friends and critics, she is sometimes nice, sometimes not so nice. She can stand up to scrutiny just like the rest of us.

But Gwen Frostic is, unquestionably, extraordinary. She and everything she has done is remarkably unique, a testimony to her intelligence and ironclad independence. Solitary and sure, she has made every one of her own decisions, often against advice and custom. Her accomplishments are an inspiration—for women, for seniors, for business people, for all of us who hope to accomplish something on our own.

Gwen Frostic, you might say, is one of Michigan's Centennial Citizens. And this is the story of her life.

Learning to Walk One Fall at a Time

The baby was as hot as a cast iron stove. The young mother clutched the child and paced the wooden floor in the silent night, her eyes dark with worry. Every now and then, when she grew too exhausted to go on, the baby's father took over.

It was Christmas Eve, 1906—just past the turn of the last century—in Croswell, a rural town in Michigan's thumb. The scene was a rented, wood frame house right in town where Fred Frostic, then just 26, could walk to the local school, where he was principal.

But school had been far from Fred's mind that Christmas week. The baby's fever had persisted for days. Her frantic young mother, Sara, had tried everything she could: cold compresses, alcohol baths, prayers. Aspirin was relatively new then and not common in most of Michigan's rural medicine cabinets. People had always used willow bark, from which aspirin derives. But no one today knows whether Sara, then only 21, had either of those medicines. If she did, they also failed.

In 1906, there just wasn't much she could do as her second born, Sara Gwendolen—nicknamed Gwen—cried in feverish pain. Except pace. This Sara and Fred did, day and night. They must have assumed, almost expected, their baby would die—an occurrence parents faced regularly in 1906. They mourned the possible loss of this especially spirited child. So bright, so full of energy! She had already begun walking. She had beautiful auburn curls, bright, curious eyes and a smile that charmed her father's heart.

It certainly crossed Fred and Sara's minds to photograph their sick little girl as the situation grew more grave. Parents often photographed their terminally ill children to preserve their memory in family history—a poignant tradition of the times. Such photographs from that era show children in bed but dressed in their Sunday best, or looking obviously ill.

But suddenly, after about a week, Gwen's fever left as quickly and mysteriously as it had advanced. Fred and Sara were relieved and thankful. But they soon noticed that Gwen could not walk as she had before, and that her motor control seemed affected.

Local doctors could not diagnose Gwen, so Fred and Sara took her to Detroit. They took the Port Huron–Northwestern rail line to Port Huron, then an electric rail car into Detroit, and then a streetcar to the office of a medical specialist.

The word "polio" was not mentioned that day in early 1907, according to Helen Warren, Gwen's sister, who is 91 and lives in Dearborn and remembers asking her mother about Gwen's illness. The specialist told Fred and Sara to get Gwen kindergarten-style equipment for what today would be called physical therapy. He told Sara how to give Gwen massages to stretch her muscles.

Fred and Sara went back home with such advice, but no real diagnosis. At some point after that, it was assumed that Gwen had had a mild case of polio. And that is what Gwen has always said, with little fanfare.

But no one will ever know what plagued Gwen that week—a reflection of the era's narrow medical knowledge and Gwen's own refusal to elaborate. In 1906, there were more questions than answers about many serious diseases. And in the plain cotton truth of the times, patients either died or they didn't. Not much else mattered because the next disease—the flu, pneumonia, an infected cut—could kill just as readily the next week. When it comes to her illness, Gwen Frostic reflects, as much as anything, such early 1900s attitudes. What was the point in analyzing?

Today, we can only guess what changed Gwen's physical appearance and, as a result, the course of her life. Was it polio? Cerebral palsy? High fevers in infant polio victims were not common, and severe illness in infants can cause cerebral palsy, we know today. Gwen still maintains she had polio and has never bothered with any newer medical tests that might shed more light on the subject.

What was more important, as the baby Gwen began to grow into a child, was how the physical after-effects of her illness would alter her life. This, of course, would be determined in large measure by how Fred and Sara reacted to their daughter's condition; special education and a more enlightened understanding of disabilities was decades away.

One incident especially reveals Fred and Sara's attitude about their "handicapped" daughter. Gwen's youngest sister, Margaret Schweitzer, 71 and a resident of Maryland, talked with Fred about Gwen's illness in the late 1940s. Margaret, 21 years Gwen's junior, spent a lot of time with an older, more reflective Fred after the rest of his eight children were grown. Margaret had just finished college and had studied special education.

"Papa," Margaret said, "I don't think it was polio Gwen had."

"Oh?" Fred replied. "And what do you think it was?"

"Cerebral palsy," Margaret said. Gwen lacked "continuous motion," indicative of that disability.

"You may be right," Fred admitted, recounting the 1906 non-diagnosis.

Margaret wanted to know more. Her father told her that Gwen had started walking at eight months old, just before she took sick.

"When did she walk again?" Margaret asked.

"What do you call walking?"

"When you get somewhere on your two feet."

"We called it walking," Fred Frostic said, "when she could go from one place in the room to the other on her feet, regardless of how many times she fell down."

Fred and Sara Frostic, it turned out, were especially suited to raise a child who was, at least in perception, handicapped. "Mama and Papa"—as their children called them—were and still are the two most important people in Gwen's life.

Fred Frostic was a small man with an oblong face, kind, intelligent eyes, and a gentle understanding smile. He was born in 1880 in Lexington, located east of Croswell on Lake Huron, in a family of several boys. His father, a shoemaker, moved the family to the Croswell area when Fred was very young. Fred graduated from Lexington High School and earned a teaching certificate from Michigan State Normal College, now Eastern Michigan University. He taught at least one year at what was known as the "Brick School House" in Lexington before taking his principal's job in Croswell in 1905.

An endlessly curious man, Fred was the dreamer in the household, the distracted professor always pursuing new interests. His work, education, was his first passion, but he found time for other passions, especially the study of Michigan nature—a passion his daughter would adopt. He loved Michigan's geology and native plants. He knew the Latin names for flowers, shrubs and trees, and taught these names to his children. He created beautiful back yards. In his long career as a teacher and administrator, he wrote several books and articles, including works such as "Early American Spellers," and "How Do You Buy Your Coal?" His 1923 book, *The Pupil's Workbook in the Geography of Michigan,* began with a foreword describing a little boy's discovery of a fossil in his back yard. This discovery helped him understand that you need not travel to exotic lands to witness the beauty of creation, and that "Michigan is a great state in which to live." The little boy was him.

Fred Frostic also took to photography, wood carving, map making and art work, which graced the Frostic household. He built furniture, played guitar and read a lot of Rudyard Kipling. In 1950, Gwen said of her father, "His hobby is what he is doing at the moment."

Though Fred was in every way a traditional father—he did not cook or clean and was frequently tied up in business away from the house—he was not the disciplinarian. He didn't really have the stomach for spanking, for instance.

His wife had no compunction about such matters. She spanked on occasion, or otherwise kept her family—which eventually included nine children—in line. "Mama did the discipline," Gwen recalled. "She never said, 'Wait till your father comes home.'" Likewise, her children never told her they were bored, "or she would find plenty for you to do."

"Mrs. Frostic, she was the boss," said Emerson Mehlhose, who would befriend the Frostics when they moved in 1918 to Wyandotte. "When she'd get on that back porch and call, they'd come, no argument."

Once, in 1919, Mehlhose recalls, Sara had to take the "steam engine" home from Detroit because the interurban couldn't operate. The train did not stop at Wyandotte—but it did after Sara talked to them.

Sara also helped Fred, a superintendent in Wyandotte, by arranging for substitute teachers. Finding subs was a real chore, so "if the women didn't show up for work, boy, they heard about it," Mehlhose said.

Sara Frostic was born in Greenleaf, near Croswell, in 1884. She also graduated from Lexington High School and earned a teaching certificate after Michigan Normal College's two year program. She taught at least one year of school.

In the Frostic household, Sara ran the ship. She was hard-headed, practical, stubborn, bright and at times wholly irreverent of convention—all qualities abundant in Gwen today. She was an excellent cook and seamstress. "Mama could make anything out of anything," Helen recalls. Helen also remembers her mother's uncanny ability to spot four-leaf clovers while hanging out the laundry. Often, the children would come in from school to find a small vase bearing a bouquet of four-leaf clovers. Helen searched in vain for what seemed like hours the same grass and came up empty.

Sara had a kind of drill sergeant approach to family. The Frostics were not sentimental people, they were not prone to confide in one another or to commiserate. No one today who ever knew the Frostic family can quite figure them out. They had very strong bonds but they weren't necessarily close. Family photographs are rare and Sara, in particular, avoided them.

As far as Sara was concerned, children were to be loved but not necessarily coddled. Helen doesn't remember being kissed, though she always felt loved. Margaret has conflicting memories of burying her face into her mother's comforting lap and her mother's order to stop crying "or I'll give you something to cry about."

Like so many people 100 years ago, the Frostics didn't whine, they worked, they didn't wish, they accepted what was and worked hard to achieve their goals. At the same time, Sara, especially, instilled into all of her children the unshakable conviction that nothing is impossible with enough hard work. All of her surviving children vouch for this. And no one could have better understood this concept than a little girl who learned to walk one fall at a time.

"I never knew I couldn't do something," Gwen has often said.

Gwen spent her first four years in Croswell. The world her bright eyes and mind examined has all but vanished, but these make-do times shaped Gwen. Croswell had fewer than 1,000 residents. Like most small towns—and many medium and larger towns—the streets were dirt, most of the traffic on them four-footed, and most houses modest and wood frame. There were no house addresses yet; residential postal delivery had not yet begun.

Croswell, surrounded by farms, had a general store, a farm machinery vender, one hand-pumped fire-fighting machine, the Helm House hotel, and A.B.'s Drug Store. Though there had at one time been a small hospital in Croswell, it had closed, and the more usual practice was for doctors to come to homes, where they performed surgery on kitchen tables as necessary. Gwen most likely visited her Uncle Lou's barber shop and her grandfather's shoemaker's shop in town. Lou Frostick, who never dropped the K from the English name, lived all his life in

Croswell, and rode a bike to work—which is still in the possession of a Croswell resident. An elementary school today is named after Lou, who was on the school board for many years.

The small-town Michigan of Gwen's childhood featured carriage houses, not garages, horse-drawn plows and farm wagons selling goods at market squares on Saturdays. People walked a lot more than they do today, and much further. Lou told of a story when he at age 12 in about 1890 had to walk 17 miles to take his family's cow from their home in Lexington to their new home in Peck, just outside of Croswell. Though this was some years before Gwen was born, the automobile had yet to transform life by her childhood years. Lou's story, published in a 1962 Croswell history, shows just how different the world of Gwen's childhood was from that of her old age.

"I left home just after sun-up, leading the cow with a rope. The road was rough and the cow, heavy with calf, wanted to rest every little while. I managed to get well over the Buel hill...but she insisted upon lying down, so I let her rest for a time; then started on again. This was just after we had passed....a farm. A Mrs. Sturges lived there then. She came out of the house and called, 'Little boy, you must be hungry and tired and your cow must be hungry, too. Come back and let me feed and water your cow and give you something to eat.'

"I did and Mrs. Sturges fed the cow and gave her some water; then she put a good meal on the table for me, but I didn't eat. I was too bashful.

"But the cow must have been refreshed as she showed less opposition until I had almost reached Peck's corners, when she decided she had had enough. She turned in the opposite direction. I had the rope around her horns and pulled back as hard as I could, but she dragged me several rods before she gave in, and I managed to turn her around and head to Peck...to the Stock's place. It was dark then. They put me up for the night in the front spare room in a nice clean bed. The next morning I walked into town to my father at his shop. I was a pretty tired little boy."

Everyday life, rural, isolated and modest, had changed little by the time Gwen was a youngster. In early 1900s Croswell, women still wore long dresses and went to their mothers' homes to give birth. Sara had done just that for her first born, Kenneth, in 1904, and for Gwen, who joined Michigan's population April 26, 1906. Both were born at their grandmother Alexander's house just up the road in Sandusky, the Sanilac County seat named after the Ohio town. Sandusky, much like Croswell, was a hopeful little farming village with about 1,000 residents and a fine, three story Victorian Courthouse that cost $20,000 to build, according to local histories. It would burn in 1915.

Though the first autos had already appeared on America's main streets, trains—the railroad—still ruled. It was a feather in a town's cap to get a railroad stop and Croswell had fought hard for that honor in 1879—which made Fred and Sara's trip to Detroit easier 28 years later.

Gwen of course did not remember her first trip to Detroit, when she was so ill, but it bore no resemblance to today's metropolis. As Fred and Sara jostled in the street-car down Woodward or Jefferson that day in 1907, they would have seen a bustling but still contained city of mostly lower level buildings—no more than about six stories. The city's only two skyscrapers were the Hammond and Majestic Buildings, 14 and 10 stories, and they were regarded by citizens with amazement. Virtually none of the city's architectural gems had been built. The Frostics would have seen an occasional Ford Model A or Oldsmobile spitting down the street, but far more horses, wagons and carriages. But the city, full of embryonic automobile factories, would soon explode in growth and prosperity.

The world's first concrete-paved mile was laid on Woodward two years after Fred and Sara made this visit. Detroit's first auto show would occur in 1910—when steering wheels were still on the right hand side of cars. But its earlier roots and remnants of horse-and-carriage Detroit—Victorian homes and river-dominated industry—was still apparent in the "electric light poles" around town, the cedar block-paved streets, the old elm trees that lined Woodward Avenue, the spacious homes on Jefferson.

Detroit would play a much larger role in Gwen's life than Croswell, although she never lost her affection for small towns and rural areas, where she chose to live most of her life.

In 1910, Fred Frostic was hired as superintendent of schools in St. Charles, another small, farm town located on the Bad River just southwest of Saginaw, where he would remain for eight years. It was a bigger Frostic family that moved to St. Charles. During her last years in Croswell, Sara had given birth to Helen in 1908 and Frederick Ralph (called Ralph) in 1909. Each child's name was added to the family Bible in Fred's artistic script.

The St. Charles "schools"—all twelve grades—were located in one big brick building. It had a bell tower the janitor rang from the third grade room. If the janitor saw a student rushing in late, he kept ringing. One man in town still remembers seeing Fred Frostic lean out of his second story window telling him to get off the fence.

St. Charles histories from that time show horses pulling early autos mired in muddy streets beneath single electric street lights. Women in long dresses stand on street corners near horses and carriages. There were several saloons, a pool room and ball alley, a tailor, barber, dry goods store, milliner shop, general store and tea store.

Merchants sold tin ware, buggies, wagons and phonographs. The Justice of the Peace was located upstairs of Charles Peters' saloon and the post office was at the drug store. A local saw mill and a coal mine, which once loaded 600 tons of coal in one day, provided employment outside of farming. The Frostics, Gwen recalls, lived within walking distance of this business district, though they kept a horse and buggy.

Gwen reached school age in St. Charles. This was a time when "handicapped" children were almost hidden at home, and certainly not educated in public schools. But Fred the educator and Sara, the hard-headed non-conformist, sent Gwen to school with the rest of her siblings—who kept coming during the family's St. Charles years: William was born in 1910, Donald in 1913 and Andrew in 1917.

Sending Gwen to school was especially challenging since she could not walk well. But it was not for lack of practice. Since her early, post-illness days when she fell more than walked across rooms, Gwen was sent out with her siblings to play pom-pom-pullaway and tag on her own power. Her siblings were not allowed to help her when she fell. One can only imagine the scene: a determined little child running with punctuated falls all over the rural yards of Croswell and St. Charles.

But Fred and Sara did make some quiet allowances for Gwen's disability. Helen remembers being told that Gwen "wouldn't be around very long," probably a reflection of what doctors then believed. Helen was never formally assigned to be Gwen's protector but she always felt that way and her parents probably did not discourage this. They sent Helen to school one year early to help Gwen.

"When I went to kindergarten, they assigned me to take Gwen, because they couldn't trust Kenneth," Helen said. "I was what they called spunky. Gwen was in first grade. I took her to school in a sulky," a small, two-wheeled cart. "We pulled it."

Gwen always emphasizes that she was like any other child. Not exactly, especially in the eyes of others. Helen remembers other children routinely coming up to her asking, "What's the matter with your sister?"

"Nothing," the scrappy Helen would reply. "What's the matter with *you*?" Many assumed Gwen had "St. Vitus'

Dance," a temporary neurological disorder that affects motor control.

The automatic description of Emerson Mehlhose, the childhood friend Gwen knew a short time later in Wyandotte is a good example of how Gwen was viewed by other children.

"Well of course, she was crippled," Mehlhose said when asked about his memories of Gwen. "That struck us when we were little. But we didn't treat her as anything but one of us."

Gwen, who was something of a tomboy compared to the more ladylike Helen, "couldn't control her head, her walk was different, she kind of dragged a foot along." But Gwen, he and the others knew, never invited pity.

Privately, Helen and her siblings understood that Gwen's illness—which the family simply never discussed— had left her sister unable to grasp a pencil well, to walk completely straight, to speak without a slight slur. None of these physical effects actually prevented Gwen from doing most things, but her handicapped appearance marked every person's first impression of Gwen—and still does. Gwen learned early to either ignore what the other children said about her, or to deny altogether that she was different—all the while proving over and over she was equal if not superior to her peers, something of a vicious circle. When she asked her mother why she wasn't invited to a party once, her mother told her bluntly to get used to it. The defenses such experiences encouraged in Gwen would develop into a full-blown character trait—some liken it to a giant chip on her shoulder—that affected her relationships the rest of her life.

It must have been especially difficult for Gwen to be constantly underestimated because she was highly intelligent; she would be placed in gifted programs today. As a very young child, her mother, perhaps in exasperation, once told Gwen she was "feeble-minded," a word commonly used then in connection with the handicapped. Gwen, to her mother's surprise, marched over to the dictionary in the Frostic home, looked up the word, marched back to her mother and announced, "I am not!" This would not be the first time Gwen would go out of her way to prove people wrong.

The next time she did so was at school. Teachers told Sara that Gwen's stiffened hands would prevent her from learning to write. Gwen, mentally stubborn and artistically inclined, proved them wrong. She had spent uncounted hours practicing threading needles and gripping pencils at home. Sheer determination produced impressive results: Gwen developed a flowery, controlled script that one day would be a recognized Michigan trademark.

Such experiences taught Gwen to rely on her own abilities and to distrust, even disregard, what so-called "authorities" said, to ignore what her peers thought, to rely on no one but herself.

Gwen was different in her own right as well. She seemed instinctively to challenge the way things were normally done, never relying on previous traditions unless they made sense. She had unusual interests for a girl. She liked playing with blocks, and later hammers and saws. Hardware stores fascinated her and still do. "Dolls didn't interest me," she once said. "I never got a train. I always wanted a train. The boys got trains. I always envied the freedom I saw that men had to work and accomplish things. I always wanted to control myself."

Gwen recalled, too, that art was an early interest. "I was always sketching," she said. "I was always interested in creating. I remember making guitars out of cigar boxes."

In 1917, Fred Frostic moved his family once again, this time to Ann Arbor for one year so he could earn his bachelor's degree at the University of Michigan. For once, the Frostic children pulled no weight in the superintendent's office.

"In St. Charles, we were somebodies," Helen recalled. "In Ann Arbor, we were nobodies."

That factor may have led to an incident that Helen recalls vividly and Gwen not at all. Helen's classroom was located across the hall from Gwen's in Ann Arbor. One day, Helen looked through the door windows to see Gwen's teacher shaking Gwen by the shoulders so hard, Gwen's head bobbed back and forth.

Furious, Helen stomped out of her class and over to Gwen's. She learned the teacher had accused Gwen of stealing another girl's thimble. At the time, girls were taught sewing in school as well as at home.

"I knew she didn't steal the thimble," Helen said, "because Mama could never get Gwen to wear a thimble. Gwen couldn't have cared less about a thimble. So I took her out of the room, down the stairs and took her home."

Sara was not home at the time. But when the teacher came by that evening to complain, Sara did not invite her in. They spoke on the porch. When Sara came in, neither Gwen nor Helen were punished.

The Frostics rented a house on what is now the site of a University of Michigan classroom building. Nearby stood the beautiful Michigan Central Railroad Station, built in 1886 on Depot Street in an industrial district. Today it is one of Ann Arbor's up scale restaurants, the Gandy Dancer. It was then the town's transportation hub, full of activity. Thirteen trains a day took passengers to Detroit and Chicago. Travelers, mail and freight clogged the station. University students, going home at semester breaks, slid down State Street, which ran down hill toward the station, on their trunks.

The year 1917 added American doughboys. Soldiers were training in Ann Arbor preparing to ship out to Europe. Gwen remembers watching them. And it was here that an 11-year-old Gwen saw her maternal uncle, Duncan Alexander, a medical doctor, jump off a train to say good-bye to his family. He was bound for France, and survived the war.

After Fred earned his degree, he had two job offers. One job offer was from a Kansas school. Sara was terrified of cyclones. Kansas was out. So in 1918, when Gwen was 12, her father accepted a job as Superintendent of Wyandotte Public Schools. He would remain there until he retired, beloved and respected, 32 years later.

Her Brush, Her Pencil, and Her Pen . . .

In 1918, the Frostics, nine strong, moved into an aged Victorian house at 129 (later changed to 355) Oak Street in Wyandotte, a short walk from the downtown area. They soon realized, as they took walks to and from town, that Wyandotte was, compared to Croswell and St. Charles, a city. About 13,000 people lived there. Biddle Street, the town's main avenue, had been paved since 1907 as were many residential streets. The town had four hotels, a theater house, its own electric company and power plant, a library, gas station, brewery and a bottling plant. Many townspeople worked at the fur and shipbuilding plants along the Detroit River. But even more significant as time went on for Gwen, Wyandotte was within reaching distance of Detroit.

The Frostics' green-and-yellow painted house had been built in the 1860s and belonged to the Mehlhose family, which owned the small ice cream factory next door. They charged between $30 and $45 monthly rent the entire 30-plus years the Frostics lived there. The house had two stories, a back porch, a barn out back and a coal bin in the basement. Now on Michigan's list of historic places, it was so old that when Fred installed storm windows in the 1940s, he learned that each window was a different size. The windows came to symbolize the colorful Frostic family and its experiences in this house, where Gwen grew up.

With Sara's help, Fred Frostic wasted no time transforming the small yard into a Garden of Eden. Out front was a formal English garden full of coleus, spider plants, geraniums and cannas. Dutchman pipe vine crawled up a trellis on the front porch. The east side of the house had a red bud tree, light purple lilacs and a European mountain ash tree, ringed by more flowers.

The back yard had a cement lily-pad pool. Fred dumped goldfish leftover from school into it. Many times, Margaret dropped her fox terrier into it. A large rock garden with terraces, full of flowers, ferns and catnip for the neighbor's cat filled the yard's west side.

A garden was devoted to Fred's beloved iris plants. Near the back steps were morning glories and moonflowers. There was a small Japanese-style garden, complete with a painted dish pan serving as a mini-pond. Roses were here and there, and Sara put out water and bread crumbs for the birds on a stone bench, no matter the weather—a scene her daughter would replicate, but on a much grander scale, years later. She poured water from cooking ham onto the lilies-of-the-valley by the door and they thrived.

The children were, of course, enlisted for yard care. Its physical beauty and diversity, especially in what was quite

a small area, clearly helped shape Gwen's innate apprecia-
tion of the beauty of everyday plants, trees and flowers.
Like her father, she learned that she didn't have to travel
beyond her own back yard to see nature's finest artwork.
Her artistic eye took in the fine duplication of flower pet-
als, the intricate construction of a simple bird's nest, dark
bare branches against coral skies, and the acrobatics of
ordinary squirrels. Years later, one of her first linoleum
print images was of a cardinal that frequented the Frostics'
little botanical garden.

Indoors, life was equally interesting. The Frostic children in 1918 ranged in age from Kenneth, at 14, to Andrew, only a year old. There were art projects, hobbies,
newspapers and books everywhere, people dropping by for
dinner at a moment's notice, singing around the piano,
guinea pigs and dogs—the Frostics always had a dog.

Every so often, the family roasted hot dogs by the coal
furnace in winter. Every Sunday two children had to play
bridge with Fred and Sara. Gwen hated bridge, but followed
orders. Her mother was an excellent bridge player.

Fred and Sara were amazingly tolerant of their
children's pursuits and escapades, whatever they might be.
Sara's ennui about house cleaning probably helped. Something as simple as dish washing was an adventure. Gwen
usually washed the dishes, one of the boys dried and then
threw the dishes to another brother at the pantry door. A
lot of dishes were broken.

Gwen's later soft spot for little boys may have had its
genesis at home. She had only one sister, Helen, for most

of her life at home, and her brothers were always doing the kind of things boys—and, often, Gwen herself—like to do. For a while, they decided to cook up dead animals, separated out the bones and hung them in their bedroom, achieving a custom vertebrae motif. This was led mainly by Bill, the future surgeon, who had an insatiable urge to explore physiology. Once, Sara asked Fred what the boys were doing in the kitchen. Fred waltzed into the kitchen, looked, saw a dead rat boiling away, and calmly told Sara they were just boiling water.

Another time, Gwen's little brother Ralph wrung the necks of all the family's chickens in the chicken coop. Fred hated chickens and had kept them because his father had insisted upon it. Ralph was not punished.

The parlor was the only room that was always neat in the Frostic home. This is where Fred conducted business. New teachers came by often as well. Sara spread maps on a table to help them find rooming houses.

In the living room were books, a radio and Fred's desk, where he played solitaire or diagrammed football games he heard in later years on the radio. Rugs covered the floors, lace curtains the windows. Fred had made the heavy oak furniture. Sara held card parties in this room or conducted meetings for the Garden Club, which she helped establish.

Adjacent to the living room was Gwen and Helen's bedroom. It was so small their double bed touched three walls. The dining room had a side porch, used by the milkman, egg man, grocery man, laundry man and the school truant officer, Nelson Hedrick, who often came by to tell Fred about poor families in need.

The dining room was more ornate, a 20-faced crystal prism in the window that "flooded the room with rainbows," Margaret later recalled. On the walnut dining room table, Sara piled clothes for the needy.

The kitchen had lots of shelves but no cabinets, typical for its day. There was an icebox and a gas stove with curved legs, beneath which Sara set bread to rise. This was also where the dog usually slept.

Also in the kitchen, Helen recalled, was Gwen's special drawer full of art supplies—many of them vendor's samples Fred brought home from school. Helen remembers this chiefly because she did not have such a drawer. But Gwen's talent had been obvious early. She seemed never to be without a drawing pad and pencil. Her sisters and brothers learned that if they needed a picture, they need only ask Gwen, who always obliged them.

Creative and independent, Gwen thrived in this suit-yourself household. "Growing up in a big family trained me to think quickly," she once said. "If you didn't, you missed your chance. I never remember saying, 'I wish I'd thought of that.'"

No project was too unusual, especially if you did it yourself. Outside the house, Gwen always faced the perception that she was somehow different and, by definition, less capable. But at home, she could do most anything she set her mind to.

These two factors encouraged Gwen's already strong maverick tendencies. Rather than trying to fit in, Gwen was entirely comfortable in going her own way; perhaps she had by then understood that no matter what she did, she would always be initially perceived as handicapped. She felt no need to follow the crowd, no pressure to follow trends; what good would it do? She considered conformity as proof only of mediocrity. Years later, she would scold Margaret for wanting to be like other girls. "Why would you want to be like everybody else?" she asked, mystified.

As the oldest girl at home, however, Gwen had to assume some domestic duties. By high school, she did all the baking. She made a delicious fig pudding at Christmas. She loved chocolate, especially chocolate-covered peanuts, and Coca-Cola. She did what was necessary with her brothers and sisters. But if she was excessively maternal, no one remembers it, although her brother, Don, now 85 and in ill health, said "you could take your troubles to her and she'd listen."

"Gwen always thought of Gwen," said Garnet Frostic, Don's wife, in an interview shortly before she died in August, 1998. "She always has done pretty much what she wanted." Garnet, who married Don in 1938, believes that Fred and Sara in some ways pampered Gwen because she had been so ill. But, at the same time, "you did not sympathize with her. You never said, 'You shouldn't do that.'"

Farms still surrounded Wyandotte back in the early '20s. What is now Southgate was then Ecorse Township, full of cornfields. Sara often gave her children a nickel each to take the streetcar about four miles south to Grosse Ile, then still a naturalist's wonderland, where they picked wildflowers. The children would buy an ice cream with the money instead and walk all the way to Grosse Ile and back. Gwen walked this eight miles right along with her sisters and brothers, unhampered by her slight limp.

Along with this more rural beauty was the urban presence of Detroit, which Gwen later credited for giving her a sophistication she would not have gained in St. Charles. Ironically, day trips into the city were much easier than they are today. The Frostics could go by streetcar, interurban lines, railroad or jitney.

The Frostics usually chose jitneys for their frequent family trips into Detroit. Jitneys were open-air autos that could be rented, much as taxis are today. It cost the Frostics 25 cents to get to Detroit, and the family probably filled up two jitneys, three to a seat.

The family went to Hudson's or Kern's, but more often they went to Detroit for entertainment. Masonic Temple had concerts, and every winter, Fred took his family to Orchestra Hall to see the day's finest conductors.

The Detroit that Gwen, then a young teen, saw on these trips had changed a great deal since Fred and Sara's 1907 visit. Its population had grown from about 400,000 to one million. A kind of architectural renaissance, chiefly with the leadership of architect Albert Kahn, had since about 1914 produced many of Detroit's handsome old buildings: the David Whitney, the Dime, the Woolworth Tower, the Woodward and Ford buildings, and the Michigan Central Railroad Building. Within the next five years would come the Fisher Building, the Fox Theater, the Penobscot and Buhl buildings, among others.

The automobile was now firmly in control of Detroit's future. Dozens of plants produced automobiles or auto components. The Ford Motor Company Highland Park plant, built in 1914, covered 60 acres. It included the largest building in Michigan under one roof and was the nation's first auto assembly line. Detroit was pure energy.

Too young to go to either Grosse Ile or Detroit with her siblings was Marjorie, the lively newcomer to the Frostic family. Born in 1922, she was the eighth Frostic child. Sara was 38 when she gave birth to Marjorie. By then, she had gained weight. This was one reason she hated being photographed. She also was secretly worried about her family's history of strokes; several of her relatives had died before age 50.

Fred Frostic was busy with his new superintendent's job. The school system he had inherited in 1918 had 42 teachers and 1,128 students. But it was growing fast. Nearby Ford City, which Wyandotte would annex in 1923, added several schools to the system.

Fred, who had a very small staff, was personally involved in everything from accounting to overseeing building construction—all for $35 a week. His children remember him studying architectural drawings on the kitchen table, and he later wrote articles about the subject. The most exciting school project was the completion of Theodore Roosevelt High School in 1923—a year before Gwen graduated. At the same time, Fred earned a master's degree from the

University of Michigan in 1927, participated in several associations and taught college classes. Highly regarded and trusted, even students had kind words for him.

"He didn't drink, smoke or swear," Garnet Frostic said. "He was what public servants used to be."

Gwen prospered in Wyandotte. As she neared high school graduation, she was confident, robust, pretty. Wearing her naturally curly hair short and combed to the side, she was very short and usually dressed neatly in tailored outfits. She was, even then, organized, focused and goal oriented. She was also savvy. Helen loved Gwen's taste in clothes, so Gwen would buy things Helen liked and sell them to Helen for more than she paid for them, Helen remembered.

Gwen's 70 classmates respected her artistic talent. She used a band saw to create life size posters for school events. She did all the artwork for the 1924 "Wi-Hi" yearbook, which mentions her often.

"Her brush, her pencil and her pen will make this world a better place!" the yearbook says near her photo. The "Senior Alphabet" reads: "F is for Frostic, an artist named Gwen, who has talent for painting with brush and with pen." In mock elections that included categories such as Most Popular, Bashful, Worst Bluffer and Laziest Boys, Gwen was voted Class Artist.

But Gwen was still a maverick; unlike other girls, she took years of mechanical drawing. Her father had to help smooth ruffle feathers of the all-male staff and students. Gwen, oblivious, simply took the classes and excelled in them. She didn't care whether the teachers or other students wanted her there or not.

The yearbook detailed the activities of the Class of '24 from junior high school on and offered a peek into the social lives of young teens of that era. The students had a marshmallow roast, a burlesque show, a *Ladies Home Journal* subscription campaign (net take: $52), a masquerade party and a wiener roast, when participants "went to the park in machines" (automobiles).

By this time, Fred Frostic owned a car, a Dodge. But Gwen was not allowed to drive it; no one was. Fred's rule was that you didn't drive a car until you owned it. Margaret recalled that only the boys in her family were taught to drive, anyway. Gwen decided at some point that she would never drive—a tacit acknowledgment of her less-than-perfect motor control. This decision probably also reflected the abundant mass transit of the time.

Gwen had plenty of friends in high school, although if she had a best friend, neither she nor anyone else has mentioned a name. She had no romantic relationships. Some believe Gwen had no interest or need. Others think it more likely that because she looked handicapped, she wasn't asked on dates or to dances. Helen recalled that a boy named Bill was "very fond" of Gwen, and that Gwen was fond of him. But Helen also believes Fred and Sara quietly protected Gwen to discourage any potential heartbreak.

"Besides," Helen said, "Gwen was smarter than most of the boys."

Gwen, at much prodding, simply has said romance "just didn't come. It didn't happen." But she did admit to at least one gentleman's invitation later, when she was attending Western Michigan University. She refused to elaborate, other than to say that the date was for a "ball game" and that "I said no."

But, as always, Gwen's "handicap" was a specter in her life, no matter what she did. One day, according to family sources, Sara took Gwen to some kind of doctor in either Detroit or in Windsor, Ontario. Gwen was probably in her teens. Emerson Mehlhose remembers the Frostics talking about that doctor's appointment. Sara may have wondered if any new medical developments could help her daughter, but no one knows what prompted this visit—only its outcome.

The doctor was blunt and rude. He told Gwen she had to face the fact that she was "different," and that she would always be different. There was nothing she could do about it.

His pronouncement deeply shook Sara, who cried. But Gwen—who almost never cried, no matter what happened—did not. Still, she must have felt a little confused. All her life, her parents had treated her like the others, told her she could do anything. Now, her mother was crying because a doctor had said Gwen was "different."

Gwen went home that day, looked at herself square in the mirror and wondered: What was so very different about her? Why couldn't people see that she was like everyone else in far more many ways than she was different from them? She realized then that she could never change what people saw in her, but that she could certainly affect what she did. It was a kind of epiphany. If Gwen ever had an inclination to win approval from others before that, she never sought such approval again.

Gwen's high school graduation day came in June, 1924, an exciting day in the Frostic house. Relatives were invited to celebrate, including Sara Frostic's sister-in-law, "Aunt Bertha." Before the graduation ceremony, Aunt Bertha insisted Gwen wear a little lipstick—a daring directive. In 1924, good girls did not wear lipstick.

"You need a little color," she declared.

Gwen's graduation capped an unusually long period of prosperity and good luck in the Frostic family. They were living in a time when poverty and disease could strike anytime; there were no government programs, no immunizations, no antibiotics. Gwen's illness had been the family's only real health crisis. But tragedy came the year after Gwen graduated.

One day, Gwen's little brother Andrew came home sick from elementary school. Before the family realized he had the measles, little Marjorie contracted the then-lethal disease. At the adorable age of 2, Marjorie died.

"It was horrible," Helen said. But not much else is known about how the family handled it. The child was laid out at the Frostic home, according to the custom of the time, and Mehlhose remembers being there with the Frostics. Gwen has vague memories and little comment about it. Margaret, born about three years later, often wondered if she was, in some way, a replacement.

In any case, Marjorie would not be the only Frostic to die young.

Following her parents' lead, Gwen "went to Ypsi," which was the family's way of saying she attended Michigan State Normal College in Ypsilanti. There Gwen studied art education from 1924 to 1926 and earned a teacher's certificate. But perhaps most important to her at the time was her acceptance into the Alpha Sigma Tau sorority. In those days, students applied for sororities at the Dean's office. And Gwen's acceptance must have signaled to her that she was accepted on equal terms with fellow classmates. She went to rush parties and then lived at the sorority house in Ypsilanti's residential district. Since the school was only a few buildings at the time, there were no dorms. Students stayed either in rooming houses or, if they were lucky, fraternity and sorority houses. About 14 or 15 women lived in the Alpha Sigma Tau house, along with a watchful housemother. Gwen made several friends at her sorority—women who recognized and then ignored her handicap.

Sorority sisters had to conduct themselves properly most of the time. There were business meetings and dinner was provided by a cook. There were two dances a year, usually held at the nearby armory. Young women had fun but remembered they were ladies. They dared not drink alcohol, smoke or curse. Alcohol would have been a little difficult for them to obtain, anyway, during Prohibition.

In 1926, Gwen decided to transfer to Western State Normal College, now Western Michigan University. Established in 1903, Western consisted primarily of three beautiful Greek Revival classroom buildings that sat like an Acropolis on a large hill. Students could climb dozens of stairs or take a small cable car, now long gone, that ratcheted up the hill.

Around that time, Western touted that it had one of the "largest Normal School gymnasiums in the old Northwest Territory." College courses included manual training, penmanship and rural education. Women and men used separate gymnasiums. Gwen's brother, Ralph, a freshman in 1926, belonged to the "Square and Compass Club." Also in '26, the year before Gwen left Western, there were 93 seniors and 7,000 alumni. Local merchants advertised in yearbooks products such as "ladies ready-to-wear" clothing and player-pianos.

Gwen lived in a rooming house and continued her art education studies. It was during these art courses that she encountered the only other person, other than her parents, who has earned her life-long admiration. Lydia Siedschlag was a fine arts professor. Two of her sketches still hang in an administration building. Gwen characteristically refused to say much about the woman, but Helen recalled that Siedschlag took a keen interest in Gwen's talent and future. She may have been Gwen's first mentor, the first instructor who focused on her abilities. The two remained friends thereafter, keeping in touch with one another. Gwen thought enough of the woman to dedicate, decades later, one of three stained glass windows she paid for at Kanley Chapel on WMU's campus. The other two are dedicated to herself and her father.

In one of her art classes at Western, Gwen carved her first linoleum block image: a monkey. But she did not pursue the craft or seem particularly interested in it.

Gwen left Western just short of a degree in 1927, which did not please her parents. Sara, 42, was grappling with infant Margaret. Business, not marriage or housekeeping, was foremost on Gwen's mind. She tried teaching art in Dearborn for one year; it did not work out, she said simply. Gwen's natural and strong instincts as an entrepreneur and artist probably overshadowed the more nurturing role of teacher. Others believe that students made fun or otherwise concentrated on Gwen's handicap, angering or hurting her.

Gwen also was bowing to reality. "I had to make a living," she said of her unorthodox decision to set up a metal shop in her parents' basement. Her father and brothers fixed up the basement for her. She would make and sell art, she decided. She called her business Metalcraft.

The pre-Depression years saw Gwen regularly going to a hardware shop on Leonard Street in Detroit, getting rides from friends or taking public transportation. There, she bought 50 or 75 pounds of 18 gauge copper and brass at a time. Using mallets, hammers and saws, she began to create beautiful things: an intricately carved copper hot plate, an exquisite dragon fireplace screen, a waist high, copper sun dial.

While making these items, Gwen also taught metal craft to small groups. She charged $15 for about 10 lessons. Her father's position as superintendent helped encourage people to take the class.

The basement became Gwen's domain and trespassers paid a price. Once, a possum got loose from her brothers and camped out in the basement for three weeks. Gwen found it amid the jellies, bashed it with a screen and told her brothers to "get that thing out of here."

Two years into Gwen's first business enterprise, the stock market crashed. Fred Frostic's stable, public school job helped shield his family from the Depression's worst effects, although Gwen's brothers lost their jobs and had trouble getting work. Margaret recalls Sara handing out plates of food to people at the back door. But Gwen remembers no particular hardship during the Depression. In fact, the effects of the crash were "quite exaggerated," she said in a remark typical of her bootstraps philosophy. "The people who jumped out of buildings were the people who bought on margin. I think that was exaggerated, too."

By this time, Kenneth was married and Helen would soon be. Ralph, Don and Andy were either in college, working or married. Bill was still single but busy as a doctor and likely looked forward one day to marriage.

Gwen had Gwen, and it seemed clear that would not change. Perhaps the two people most aware of that were Gwen herself, and Sara, the mother who sensed she would not be around much longer.

Gwen didn't worry, never showing any sign of interest in close relationships. She was married to her work, in love with it, and her dedication began to bear fruit. The next few years were good ones for her. She taught her classes and was asked by the Detroit YMCA to teach her unusual metal craft. She didn't realize it, but her reputation as an artist was spreading. One day, a woman came to the Frostic front door. Mrs. Henry Ford, the woman said, wanted two flower vases. Gwen said many years later that she made the copper vases "to fit the arrangements that she wanted to make." The woman later picked them up. Gwen charged $25 each, "what I charged everyone else," she said.

At home, Sara was in her late 40s and on the go. She was not only raising her children but active in several community organizations: First Congregational Church, Eastern Star, White Shrine, Wyandotte Garden Club, Past Patron's Club, Lizzie Schaffer Club, Tuesday Study Club and the Wyandotte Married Teachers' Club. She also chaired the State Federation of Women's Clubs on Education. This civic involvement marked her children, who all followed her example by joining various community groups and associations.

Sara kept a keen eye on her children as well, including her older children. Helen, in her early 20s, met a young man named Neil Warren. Sara decided she did not like Neil. Though he was a young architect, he didn't have a good job yet. He wasn't good enough for Helen, Sara said. Helen returned that he was plenty good enough for her.

But at the time, people tended to live with their parents until they married, and Sara did what she could to discourage Neil. Once, when Neil called Helen on the telephone, Sara answered. Is Helen there? he asked. No, Sara said. Do you know when she'll be in? No, Sara answered. Could you leave a message? No, Sara answered.

After he hung up, Helen said, "the operator gave him his nickel back."

Sara was constantly busy with these matters and with Margaret, who was only 7. She was also constantly battling high blood pressure. The doctor had given her medicine, but she stubbornly refused to take it. Gwen has vivid memories of watching her mother dump the stuff down the sink. Gwen knew what this would mean, but her mother was adamant; she would take no medicine.

The result was predictable. On January 30, 1935, Gwen came home to find her mother in her bedroom, immobile. She had had the stroke she had always worried about. She was 50. Gwen immediately called Papa.

"There was a lot of commotion," Gwen said later. "The doctor came to the house."

Sara lingered a while in the hospital, semi-conscious. On February 2, Gwen woke up her little sister, Margaret. It was the only time Margaret had seen her big sister cry. Mama had died, Gwen said, sobbing quietly.

The family grieved strangely. No one talked about Sara's death. Gwen went back to work. In the peculiar Frostic fashion, Gwen dearly loved her mother but was not close to her. The Frostics, in her words, "went their own way."

Fred—who avoided the subject of death to the point of missing his own father's funeral—said very little about his wife's death. But he mourned her, spending long, sad hours in his chair wearing his burgundy housecoat.

Fred finally went back to work and the family tried to adjust. Bill, who was living and practicing medicine in

Detroit, helped the family heal emotionally. Blessed with some of his father's easy-going nature, Bill was warm, humorous and optimistic. His presence was uplifting.

As eldest daughter, Gwen took over the domestic duties. She did not complain. "It had to be done, so I did it," was her way of explaining the situation. Only Margaret and Don, who would soon marry, were still home.

The following three years, with Gwen as a mother to young Margaret, were rather adventurous. Once, she and Gwen put down new red linoleum in the kitchen, decided they didn't like the color and painted over it. They stayed up very late at night; Gwen drank Coke and ate burned toast. One year, Gwen made Margaret a green, pink and chocolate birthday cake. She also made a silver ring with a blue stone and silver dot. The ring represented them.

In 1938, Don married Garnet and Fred, after a year courtship, married Florence Shirey, a genteel, piano-playing French teacher at Roosevelt High. Fred had waited, according to the custom at the time, two years after this wife's death before courting and remarrying. Florence took over the domestic duties, immediately noting that the Frostic household was not particularly clean.

"See? It only took an hour," she once said to Gwen after cleaning the oven. Gwen, who had by then started her stationary business, was unfazed. "In an hour, I made $40 worth of stationery," she said.

After three years taking care of home and family, Gwen was more than ready to get back to her work full time. In her late 20s, she was enjoying life. She worked hard, but she was also quite social. She had joined the Wyandotte Business and Professional Women's Club in 1937. She went with friends to Detroit's popular restaurants—the Russian Bear, the French Village, Sanders. Detroit was nearing its golden age, and it was the place to be in Michigan. Gwen loved just walking the streets of Detroit at night—waltzing by the city's architectural castles, clean streets, cars and people. She shopped at Crowley-Milners and Kerns. The streetcars were gone by then, but there were electric busses and trains and a sense of excitement and sophistication— intellectual sophistication—that Gwen loved.

Often, Gwen met her brother Bill for dinner. Though Gwen had never been particularly close to any family member, she formed a bond with Bill in the pre-war years, perhaps in part because he was still single. He was the only sibling she ever felt so close to.

"Every spring, he would call and say, 'Let's go find spring,'" Gwen recalled of those years. "We'd head south until we found the first robin, and then we'd come back."

Gwen, now an accomplished young woman and entrepreneur, was articulate, entertaining company. She had a great command of current issues, an opinion on most anything and a sharp, at times impish sense of humor.

"When we were first married," Helen said, "she bought us an enormous bag of canned goods—with all the labels torn off. We never knew what we were opening, and we didn't have any money."

Decades later, Gwen was still at it: she sent a large sum of money in all dimes glued to a picture to her brother

Andy, and she sent 750 pennies to Helen on her 75th birthday. She sent a $1,000 bill by regular, first class mail to a nephew as a gift. When family questioned her, she said, "You don't send anything you can't afford to lose."

In her work, Gwen had been experimenting with a new substance made by Monsanto called plastic. She used it to make the face of a beautiful copper clock. Its silver numbers were carved with a jeweler's saw.

Somehow, Monsanto learned that an artist was ordering their plastic. A representative contacted Gwen and asked her if she could make something for display in the 1939 World's Fair in New York.

Gwen brought some plastic home and went to work, with Margaret's help. It was another moment of adventure in the kitchen with Gwen, as far as Margaret was concerned. Gwen tried heating the plastic in hot water, and then in the oven. She mangled and mauled it. The end result was a beautiful tray with a copper inset and plastic outer edge carved by the jeweler's saw into morning glories.

The tray was indeed displayed at the Fair. But Gwen never saw it. "I didn't have the funds to go to New York," she later said unemotionally. She still has the tray, but "I haven't looked for it in years."

1908 – (l to r) Kenneth, Helen and Gwen

1913 – (l to r) Bill, neighbor, Kenneth, Gwen, Ralph, and Helen

1919 – (l to r) Gwen, Uncle Duncan Alexander, and
Helen in Wyandotte, Michigan

1944 – Frostics in their garden at 355 Oak Street, Wyandotte, Michigan. Front – (l to r) Bill, Gwen, Ralph. Rear – (l to r) Donald, Kenneth, Margaret, Fred W. (Papa)

Summer 1968 – Peter Schweitzer (Margaret's son)
and Gwen in the Benzonia shop

1976 – Gwen with her dog, Longfellow

1976 – Gwen with Margaret (Frostic) Schweitzer in
Gwen's Benzonia shop

I Work with Nature Because it Treats Me Equally

By late 1941, shortly after the bombing of Pearl Harbor, World War II came home to the Frostic family. Bill was the first to offer his services as a doctor in the Army Air Corps. Emerson Mehlhose will never forget the day Bill, his childhood buddy he had played ball with in the alley, came over, in uniform, to tell him he had volunteered for overseas duty. Gwen came with Bill that day, and said very little as her brother and his good friend said good-bye.

Before he shipped overseas, Bill bought a life insurance policy and listed Gwen as his beneficiary—another tacit acknowledgment of Gwen's "handicap."

Andy joined the Air Corps to serve as a dentist about two years later. Gwen, meanwhile, went to her Detroit hardware store one day to find there was no more copper; it was all going to the war effort. She could no longer make her metal craft products.

But Gwen did not worry about her livelihood then; she worried about her duty. There was a war on, and Gwen felt she had to do her part. No one expected her, a "handicapped" nearly 40-year-old woman to work the plants. She could easily have avoided that option. She never once saw it that way.

"She had two brothers who had enlisted. She felt she had to do something," Garnet Frostic said. "No one in the family wanted her to do it. She'd have to stand on street corners in the snow waiting for a ride. We didn't know she was going until she was gone. First thing we know, Gwen's going to work at the bomber plant."

The Ford Motor Company bomber plant at Willow Run near Ypsilanti was the queen of war plants. No facility better-illustrated America's industrial war might. Built in 1942, the plant covered 1,300 acres and employed identical, parallel assembly lines designed to produce one bomber every hour. The planes thundered right out of the plant to Europe. Nearby were rows of temporary housing where workers from the South lived while they worked the plants.

About half of the plant workers were women, Gwen recalls. There were also a number of dwarfs, which captured the imagination of the press. Many surviving newspaper photographs of the plant show the dwarfs with FDR and other dignitaries who toured the place.

Perched like today's sports stadium boxes above the massive plant floor were glass-walled offices. There worked the engineers, the accountants, the technical staff, their desks overlooking the giant bombers. Gwen was among them.

She worked as a tool and die drafts person—one of very few women doing so. She had first applied for the machine shop, but was rejected. Gwen designed tools needed in the plant. When something went wrong on the line, she had to troubleshoot and fix it. This required frequent trips onto the plant floor, where Gwen would stand in the shadows of those enormous bomber wings getting specifications and details. It also required a keen mind able to solve problems quickly. Gwen worked at the plant from 8:00 A.M. to 5:30 P.M. for $2.75 an hour, six days a week until the war ended. No one outworked her.

At first, Gwen commuted to the plant with a good friend. Then she decided to rent an apartment in a house on Packard Street in Ann Arbor. She shared rides to and from the plant with other women. If she made any lasting friends, she has never mentioned them. She was alone most nights, but never lonely—because by this time, she had begun her stationery business and she filled her nights making boxes for her products.

Gwen's business mind had wasted little time mourning her metal craft business. The metal craft wasn't all that profitable, she reasoned—she spent so much time and hard work making things that didn't wear out. Besides, if there was no metal, there was no metal.

But as Gwen worked the bomber plant, she remembered: there was linoleum. Lots of it. She remembered the monkey she had carved at Western. She knew linoleum was an old art, and was much easier than pounding metal. Even better, stationery products had to be replaced. There is some evidence, also, that either a teacher friend or Fred encouraged Gwen to try the linoleum.

So during her limited free time, Gwen found an art supply store in Detroit that sold squares of linoleum already mounted on blocks. Then she found a paper supply house, too.

Gwen's brother Ralph had loaned a man some money. The man had a used, hand fed, electric printing press in his garage. That loan plus $45 bought the press a new home in the Frostic basement.

Gwen brought the press home. She had no idea how it worked. So she took machine apart and put it back together piece by piece. Then she knew how it worked. Her first block carving was of a fish. Gwen stamped the fish onto some note cards. Presscraft Papers was born.

Gwen saw unlimited potential as she worked the old press on Sundays and made boxes on weeknights. Before long, she decided to rent the old Vick's grocery store at 200 Cedar Street in Wyandotte. She moved her single press into it, cleaned the place up and opened for business, her neat packets of note cards stacked, much as they are today, neatly and unceremoniously on plain shelves. Every weekend during the war, she worked her shop.

Before long, Gwen was printing letterhead stationery, business cards and other commercial jobs. When she could, she sketched wildlife—the cardinal, for instance—and carved the image into linoleum blocks.

V-J Day on August 14, 1945, found Gwen back at her shop, out of the bomber plant and into her own little plant. She converted the back of her shop into a one-room apartment where she and her fox terrier, Teddy, lived. It was the first time, other than in college, she lived away from her parents' home. She was perfectly happy in the Spartan living area. In fact, Gwen would never deviate from that home/shop set up from then on. It was practical, for one, since Gwen need only walk into another room to work, and down the street to shop. It also allowed her complete independence and solitude. For the first time she had total control over her home and her business.

The small living area mainly consisted of a kitchen and bedroom. It was pleasant but plain. A few of her copper products and pictures from the Frostic home were the only decorations. Gwen had little interest in buying anything else for the place.

"She was just putting all her money back into the business," said Bill Frostic, Gwen's nephew, who has worked for Gwen since the 1950s. "Her business was her whole life, the way it is now."

After two decades of Depression and war, people were glad to have normal lives again, and it must have felt good.

But the war wasn't over for the Frostics.

On August 20, Margaret, only one day shy of 18, was alone at the Frostic home, sewing. A messenger knocked at the door and asked for her parents. They weren't home, Margaret said. The messenger thanked her and went next door. Minutes later, the neighbors told Margaret that the messenger had a telegram but he could not deliver it to a minor.

Margaret called the telegram office and said her sister, Gwen, was working down at her shop and could accept the telegram. Margaret was told to bring Gwen to their office. Margaret—too young to understand what the telegram was, especially since the war was over—called Gwen.

"She knew what it was," Margaret recalled. But Gwen said nothing to her young sister.

Margaret went to Gwen's shop and the two went toward the telegram office. It was a scene Margaret will never forget. "We had to walk a long way," Margaret said. "It was warm. Gwen was not walking well, and I could see she was upset. When we got to the telegram office, they said they wouldn't give the telegram to us there, we had to go home. So we walked back to our house and they brought it, and Gwen opened it."

Reading the telegram must have been the most difficult thing Gwen had ever done. It told her that Bill Frostic, 35, was killed when his crew's plane crashed into a mountain in Hawaii. He was with a team of doctors that had finished its last medical mission in Japan. They were on their way home.

Bill's death was a great shock and loss for Gwen, who knew Bill as young Margaret did not. He was the shining success of the family, proof of the power of education—a University of Michigan graduate and surgeon who had served his country for four years. He was the amiable, balding guy who had helped keep the family's spirits up after Sara had died. He was Gwen's lunch and dinner date in Detroit, and the person with whom she drove south to find spring.

Margaret looked at her big sister, and saw that she was very upset, as she had been when Mama died.

"All that education," Gwen murmured, fighting back tears.

Bill's body was buried in Hawaii. Gwen kept her grief deep and private. Years later, in 1950, Gwen and Florence flew to Hawaii to see Bill's grave. In a 1998 newspaper interview, she mentioned she had traveled once to Hawaii. She did not say why.

Soon after Bill's death, Gwen began receiving the benefits from his life insurance policy: every month, she received a check for $42. She put every dime into her business—and, in a way, still does. In 1998, 53 years later, she was still receiving that $42 check.

Bill made Gwen his beneficiary, ostensibly, to help her avoid becoming a burden—a rather humorous notion in retrospect. Even by the time he died, Gwen was on her way to financial success. By 1951, Gwen's business was stable and growing, due completely to her own hard work and business talent. She was steadfast, smart and disciplined. She did virtually all the work at the shop, still using her original old press and one Heidelberg press, considered the Mercedes of printing equipment, which she learned to revere. She said in one later interview that she ran her own presses for 10 years. She also prepared the jobs, packed the products, cleaned up, and started all over again. She very early produced a catalog of products and sent it out, ever increasing her business volume.

Every day, she wore simple work dresses that usually buttoned or zipped up the front, and sensible work shoes. Her hair was always short, curled, and she wore glasses. She socialized with friends as she always had but she was more rigidly independent than ever. Her friendships were not always deep, nor did they last. Gwen offered entertaining, intelligent discourse and razor wit. She was at times charming, thoughtful and very generous. But friends could wither beneath her blunt, even rude remarks. Friends learned to ignore or tolerate such remarks, and many parted ways with Gwen, sometimes she with them. She developed a pattern of having one rather close friend, with whom she spent a great deal of time and attention, then kind of dropping that friend for another.

As a business entity, Gwen was beginning to attract attention: who was this lone, handicapped woman running this little shop, making these unusual stationery products? The *Detroit News Pictorial Magazine* came out to Wyandotte in the early 1950s and photographed her working her presses and waiting, unsmiling, on a customer. A national business woman's magazine featured her in 1960. Business was good, but it wasn't quite what she wanted, she explained.

"I went into printing with the intention of doing block-print stationary. My original idea was to make what we call shadow prints. But the whole thing sort of got away from me. I found myself doing all sorts of things for which I had no interest—wedding invitations, programs and so forth. The operation became a commercial job printing house. It's something like letting a camel into a tent. Pretty soon the camel is in and you are out. Job printing began to take all my time, with none left over for the sort of thing I really wanted to do."

Gwen soon saw a way to reverse that order. In 1950, Fred Frostic had retired as superintendent of Wyandotte schools. He learned of an unusual vacation development operated by the Congregational Assembly near Frankfort. Located on one square mile of wooded, hilly land between the shores of Crystal Lake and Lake Michigan, the development began in concept in 1901 as a place for congregationalists to continue their religious studies during summer. Some old cabins still in use today date back to 1906.

The lots—165 in all—are little but beautiful and cost a small fortune now. But Fred and Gwen bought five lots for a reasonable price.

"He was going to build a great big cottage," Gwen said. "My father was a dreamer. I knew he would never build it. So I said, 'Why don't you build a little one?'"

Gwen paid for the cottage materials and at times helped her father design a unique structure. Still in use by new owners, it resembles nothing of the predictable, folksy log cabins around it. Reminiscent of the modern, nature-embracing design of Frank Lloyd Wright, the cottage testifies to the artistic, architectural talent of Fred Frostic. Just 629 square feet of perfectly used space, it has a slanted, flat roof that juts out over a living room/eating area with floor to ceiling windows that bring nature indoors.

Four small rooms flow into one another and most walls don't quite reach the ceiling, lending an airy touch. Cupboards, made by Fred, are rounded. Two narrow bedrooms stand left of the living room, one with a wall that is mostly windows. A cut-stone fireplace forms the left wall in the living room.

The exterior walls are cinderblock "because that's what was available," Gwen said. There were no extras in the place. As late as 1993, when Gwen finally sold the cabin, there was only one electrical outlet. When the new owner talked of adding more, Gwen said, "You don't need any more light. Why do you want to make it fancy? It's just a cottage."

Gwen spent considerable time in this cottage, getting rides into Frankfort from friends or Fred and Florence. But the building itself was unimportant to Gwen, and still is. It was the north woods that captured her—the ability to walk out her door and steep herself in nature. Residents often saw her roaming the woods with Teddy, stopping to sketch. It was another Grosse Ile, a wild land near water.

By this time, Gwen strongly identified with this natural world, each little flower and plant following its own preordained plan. Her reverence was a logical culmination of her childhood wonder at Grosse Ile and her father's influence. Nature had become her God and her best friend. "I work with nature," she once said, "because it treats me equally."

She was never alone as long as she could walk outside. When asked about her religious views, she returned: what more proof do you need of a higher power than the majestic changing of the seasons, silver moonlight on shiny leaves, the nest of an industrious robin?

The north woods encouraged Gwen to change her business—a rare but crucial moment when the artist outbalanced the businesswoman. She decided on an unorthodox plan to simply close her Wyandotte shop in summer and operate a shop up north. That would give her more time to carve her original block prints, make more of her own stationery and perhaps do some writing.

Gwen opened up in what was once Dewey's Barber Shop, right next to a bait shop, on Frankfort's main street. It faced Betsie Bay, which empties into Lake Michigan. On the bay in town was the local swamp. To Gwen, it was a natural wonderland full of blue herons, frogs, waterfowl, cattails and wildflowers. Gwen spent about three summers in Frankfort, sharing the cottage at times with Fred and Florence, who had spent nearly 20 happy years together.

Fred Frostic was then in his 70s, and he did not have long to live. In March, 1954, while living with Florence in Ann Arbor, Fred had a heart attack. Gwen rushed to Ann Arbor to be with him. On March 28, he died in an Ann Arbor hospital. He was buried next to Sara in Wyandotte.

Fred's death left Gwen little reason to remain in Wyandotte. Only Don and Andrew were left in town with their families. Gwen began talking about making a change, Helen said.

"She said she was going to sell everything and move up north. And we all laughed. We knew she couldn't do that. And one day, she backed a truck up to the door of her shop, took all her stuff and moved up north."

Nothing in the World is so Powerful as an Idea Whose Time has Come

Frankfort, aptly named after the fort of a man named Frank, was a charming tourist town in the early 1950s, much as it remains. In summer, it swelled with tourists who shopped, swam, sunbathed or caught car ferries across Lake Michigan. In winter, the beautiful Victorian summer mansions went dark and business slowed to a crawl.

On Main Street was the tiny business district, with its typical '50s business district and personalities. There was Angelo, the first generation Italian who owned the grocery store, and Charlie, who ran the drug store with the long marble soda fountain. Olsen's Fisheries offered fresh fish right from the docks. The East Shore Hotel and the Park Hotel catered to the resort crowd.

Against this quaint backdrop a rather strange 50-year-old woman was seen limping down to the local swamp, or up to the post office with a fox terrier almost every day. She usually looked a mess—her hair awry, her brow sweaty, her dress and hands smudged—and she slurred her speech. Some people assumed the woman was a drunkard.

As Gwen and her dog, Teddy, became better known in town, more people realized that the smudges on her hands or clothes were just printer's ink, the limp was permanent and her trips to the swamps were to sketch, not stare. She may have looked funny but she was not feeble minded. In fact, she was very sharp—sharp as a migraine to some of the businessmen in town.

Gwen was operating in a man's world, though she never slowed down enough to notice that. At that time, she was Frankfort's lone female business owner, ostracized from the all-male Rotary Club and other such groups. And many Frankfort businessmen didn't take to her. They were uncomfortable with her appearance, for one. She wore little make-up, made no attempt to look "pretty" at work and her handicap only made her less appealing. Worse, she didn't seem to care one whit what they thought of her. She wasn't social, like the other women. Not deferring. She didn't smile enough.

Gwen returned the disfavor. "I don't think she had a high regard for most of the business community," said Robert Laubach, Gwen's first accountant. "I think she probably felt that their businesses ran them, they didn't run their businesses, and she was probably right."

In 1950, men were accustomed to negotiating with other men, but not with middle-aged, smart and unintimidated females. Gwen belittled salesmen mercilessly, says John Peterson, a life long Frankfort resident and former owner of the *Benzie County Patriot*. "She bargained them down ruthlessly to rock bottom prices," he said.

"If they said something patronizing, she'd cut 'em in half," agreed Jim Rogers, another long time resident and local builder who worked on Gwen's shops. "She'd say, 'If you're so smart, why aren't you rich?'"

Chances are, Gwen would have belittled any salesperson. To her, business was business. Operating alone, she had to make it work or there was nothing else. When customers asked her in her later years if she still worked, she answered: "I'm still eating." It was the kind of response most people her age would understand.

But her single-mindedness and her blunt remarks earned her male enemies. Peterson and several other men in town saw Gwen as a bitter, man-hating, self-centered woman—critical and downright mean. Another man who worked for her described her as having the "disposition of a rattlesnake."

Gwen's relationships with women were much stronger. She also worked at them harder. As in Wyandotte, she was active in several women's groups, most notably the P.E.O., and she gradually created a circle of women friends who loved her products and her company at lunch or dinner. Gwen's chief social activities outside of work were going out for meals and taking drives with her friends, her nephew, Bill, or her assistant at work.

Gwen enjoyed her friends' company, but she also understood networking long before businesswomen learned that skill in the 1980s. She was interested in making friends, but she was more interested in making profits. And she did. Not long after moving to Frankfort, she moved to a slightly larger, though still very small shop down the street. Frankfort residents witnessed what Wyandotte had: a middle-aged, handicapped woman working alone or with minimal help at press equipment in a little shop.

In that shop hung a sign on the wall with the well-known phrase: "Nothing in this world is so powerful as an idea whose time has come." Gwen was sure she had such an idea. Her products were now what she had always wanted them to be and so was her business. As she once described it: "Everything I do is me." And everything was for her, her way. "I don't do anything for an effect," she said. "I do it to be functional."

"We never had a salesman," Gwen said years later. "Every improvement came out of the business. We buy basic-colored inks and do our own mixing. We set our prices to make a decent profit. I have never priced competitive lines and I don't know or care what they charge. I design everything. I do a pencil sketch from life—animals, birds, plants—trace it on the block and excise it for the press. Every vein in every leaf is true to life."

Gwen selected the weight and color tone of the paper and devised a unique feathered edge that still marks her stationary products and books. She then made and sold her creations her way. Products had no glaring exterior packaging with exclamation points and promotional slang. They didn't even have prices. They were simply covered in sheer plastic and set on plain wood shelves. It was unique marketing. It was also very cheap marketing. Gwen must have understood early that packaging was superfluous. Why promote something people are already looking at? Why should you tell them what they can plainly see? Why distract from your product with glitzy shelving or advertising?

Gwen's business was especially geared toward summer tourists, who developed benign, part sympathetic, part worshipful images of her based mainly on brief, over-the-counter interactions and her endearing products; the person who could create such cute frogs and charming geese, such beautiful wildflowers, could not be hard-edged. People took those images of the sweet, handicapped artist home, along with her products, spreading Gwen's market and image. Before long, Gwen was sending catalogs to other states, establishing a mail order business that exponentially increased her distribution and her profits. She told Laubach that her business was increasing 50 percent a year.

She put that money right back into Presscraft Papers. She bought another Heidelberg Press, then another, added onto the back of the little shop, then added on again. She built a second-level apartment. She hired employees. She also began quietly to give donations to groups or individuals, but she was secretive about it and snappy when people asked her about the subject. She once gave Jim Rogers a large donation, telling him to give it to a local church but to keep her name anonymous.

Meanwhile, she managed, on a tiny wedge of grass between her shop and the gas station next door, to feed up to 150 Eastern Evening Grosbeaks at a time. Like her mother before her, only to a much greater degree, Gwen reveled in feeding birds, one of her unadvertised soft spots. Buckets of feed were set out, more and more birds stopped by to dine. It was quite a sight. It was also, to some in town, just another Gwen Frostic nuisance; they didn't care for the droppings all over downtown.

Gwen spoiled her dog as well. She fed him on demand all kinds of dog and human food, such as cookies. She would do the same for Emerson, her next dog, Longfellow, the dog after that, Von Heidelberg, another dog, and Eliot, her current dog. Gwen always had just one dog at time, she has said, because "one dog is a member of the family and two dogs is two dogs."

Gwen was less inclined to spoil her employees, who began to multiply by the early 1960s. "There were no coffee breaks and no vacation," said Ron Conklin, now an artist, who worked for Gwen at the time. "Pay was usually as minimum as she could get away with." Employees didn't kill time and were told there was no talking on the job. Gwen had no problem firing people but, one person observed wryly, "she was never stupid enough to fire someone she needed."

"She hired a lot of women," Conklin said. "They would come in starry-eyed and leave a little wiser."

Gwen would warm up to particular employees, such as Conklin, and then cool off, the same cycle she experienced with many friends. No one has been able to explain these cycles. "She had favorites and then falling out with favorites," Conklin explained. It is entirely possible that Gwen simply got bored with people and moved on. She had high standards; conversations with her could feel like mental chess matches and Gwen was always the winner, calculating many moves ahead of her opponent.

Underlying Gwen's sarcasm or critical remarks was a kind of intellectual superiority. People are different from one another, and some are better, smarter than others, she believed. That isn't bad or good, that's just the way it is.

"If you are going to divide people at all, you have to divide them between the thinkers and the non-thinkers," she said in 1986. "You can tell the difference the moment they come in by their eyes and what they look at. I know if I want to spend 10 minutes with them or say 'Hello, it's a nice day,' or just move on and not speak to them at all."

Conklin and other employees recognized Gwen's shortcomings, but they knew that no one worked harder than Gwen and that Presscraft Papers was a good, clean place to work. Gwen expected employees' entire attention and devotion on company time, but she never intruded on a person's private and personal time. There was a line and she implicitly honored it.

Evelyn Argue cleaned Gwen's shop and later her Benzonia place. She observed a woman who woke and went to bed with her business. By the time Argue arrived in the morning, Gwen already had been on the job for a while. Argue saw her tending to four presses at once. She saw a woman who could make her employees laugh with apt, humorous remarks and a woman who could get extremely mad. Gwen quietly loaned employees money, and not so quietly criticized their work at times.

One April Fool's day, Evelyn played a joke on Gwen—rushing into her office to report the death of one of Gwen's squirrels outside, which she religiously fed. At Gwen's alarm, Argue said, "April Fools!" Evelyn was not sure how Gwen would react. But Gwen's sense of humor matched her temper. She laughed.

Gwen respected her customers, for the most part, often sharing a quote she had once seen: "A customer is never an interruption of your work; he's the reason for it." But she could also be sharp-tongued behind the counter. "She could insult the hell out of people and they would laugh and laugh," Conklin recalled. They thought she was kidding or, more likely, tolerated the insults because they thought she was handicapped. Gwen understood this entirely.

Conklin was among a handful of employees who might have learned Gwen's unique trade, someone who could help carve new blocks—difficult, slow and painstaking work—or even, eventually, allow Gwen to retire. Such a person could carry on her legacy after she died. But Gwen never once broached the subject of apprenticeship. She kept her craft to herself, laboring at a simple draftsman's table at night in her apartment, wrapping her stiffened hands around her worn, wood-handled carving tools, slowly scraping beautiful images into those linoleum blocks. It could take hours to do one flower petal just right. It was an especially difficult occupation for Gwen's hands, which had been perhaps most affected by her illness. But it was also an oddly appropriate one for her personality: in order to produce clean, simple images, she had to cut away what was not needed. Gwen made this old craft her own, and began to get invitations to explain why she carved blocks, what she hoped to accomplish with her business.

"Cutting the block is the most important part," Gwen told one art class in the 1960s. "It has to be cut backward because it prints directly on the paper to be sold. I never have to finish any block at a certain time. When you do that, your work becomes dead. I sat beside everything at the time I sketched it, even if it was only a blade of grass. This makes the difference. I'm not making something for a card or book, I'm trying to create that thing.

"My job is not to educate but to help people feel the beauty of nature," Gwen went on. "I don't tell of the destruction of Lake Erie because everyone knows that. I try to get them to feel the need for beauty and the need for everything to live for us to live. This is more basic.

"Everyone in the creative field has the responsibility to do his part to prevent the destruction of nature. We must try to get people to think differently rather than do differently. The problem is deeper than going around picking up beer cans."

Gwen began to bloom as a writer in Frankfort, in part by mistake. She was for a time on the state board of the National Federation of Business and Professional Women's Clubs. ("I was the best board member they had," she often said. "I was always bored.") Gwen essentially disliked working in groups. "When a person joins a mob, he gives up his individuality just like the trees in a cluster," she once said.

"Man was made to think alone." Another way she put it: "The camel was designed by a committee." During one local businesswoman's meeting in Frankfort, when the group was discussing a plan of action to help the city, Gwen remarked: "I know what we can all do: We can go back to work," after which she promptly got up and did just that.

But Gwen remained active in the groups for camaraderie and business. And in 1957, she was asked by her fellow Federation board members to write a book the group could sell to raise funds. Gwen agreed, and that year produced her first book, *My Michigan*. The title and contents could have been written by Fred Frostic himself.

> *A flash of color in the budding trees ....*
> *... the warblers are passing through*
> *Song sparrows — bluebirds — and bobolinks*
> *sing melodies that the whole world may*
> *know the joy of simple love ......*
> *The quiet of the swampland is broken by*
> *the chatter of wild geese ....*
> *gulls talk and laugh among themselves*
> *... and the great blue heron*
> *stands sentinel of it all ...*

> *Birds ....*
> *from the tiniest hummingbird —*
> *to the greatest eagle ...*
> *somehow have a mysterious power*
> *to set our spirits free ......*

Gwen assumed the book was just a public relations tool, destined for back desk drawers. But people liked it. They liked the dry grip of the heavy pages, the unique pastel shades, the lyrical blue herons, the winking frogs, the pigeon-toed geese. They liked Gwen's view of nature and of life. The book caught on. Gwen was surprised. "My father was a writer and it never occurred to me to write until after he died," she said years ago, adding: "I think you should reach a certain maturity before you write."

Though her books would evolve some, *My Michigan* was the prototype of a product that, like its author, was difficult to classify. Visually, Gwen's book was a hybrid; prose sprinkled like poetry on thick, deckle-edge paper illustrated here and there with Gwen's unique block print nature images. Some pages were blank. None were numbered. The book bindings were plain but attractive, hard but not too hard. The subject was always nature-related and titles were simple and at times ponderous: "Ruminate," "Contemplate," "A Place On Earth," "Wing-borne," "The Enduring Cosmos," "The Infinite Destiny" and "The Evolving Omnity."

Gwen searched 18 months looking for the definition of the word "omnity." She finally found it, at the suggestion of a New York City librarian, in Webster's Second Edition. The word dated back to 1595 Italy and meant exactly what Gwen thought it meant: "everything and all."

Gwen's writing was from the beginning very personal and important to her. She reached deep into herself and, in a sense, shared far more of herself in her books, which would number 22 by 1999, than she ever did in person.

Not long after *My Michigan*, Gwen produced her second book, *A Walk with Me*, which remains one of her favorites. As she describes a walk through various natural settings, the book reveals Gwen's deep thinking and her reverence for nature's simplicity. Her prose conveys her belief that nature has all the answers and that we are part of that nature, no matter how often we forget it:

> *"Let's just wander here and there —*
> *like leaves floating in the autumn air*
> *and look at common little things —*
> *stones on the beach —*
> *flowers turning into berries ......*
> *...... from the winds we'll catch a bit*
> *of that wondrous feeling that comes —*
> *— not from seeing —*
> *but from being part of nature —*

Gwen praises "the most beautiful browns" of mushrooms, and the "in-between lands"—swamps, now called wetlands, the swaying strength of a bird's nest in strong winds, the beauty of death:

> *There is something mysteriously*
> *beautiful about a dead tree*
>
> *— as it stands no longer resisting*
> *the winds that strip its bark*
> *and twist its trunk .....*

In sunshine — rain — or snow —
it seems to suggest a power
long after life has gone ....

Just stand on the bluffs overlooking a lake, she writes,

Out where the sky begins —
and white clouds form
Soon a gull drifts by in the wind — and little
sandpipers appear on the beach below ....
.... and you are not alone

A simple walk outside will make anyone realize "How much a part of everything you are...how much all things are part of you...."

Gwen was inspired by her father and her love for nature, but she also modeled her style in part on an old brown book that still sits on her desk as it probably has for decades. *At the Turn of the Year: Essays and Nature Thoughts* was published in 1913.

The book itself contained similar prose, deep thinking, image-heavy and inspirational. It is typical pre-World War I innocence and hope and it is integral to Gwen's own philosophies:

"Just as the waving hand of the sun beckons the white, wandering clouds, as the shepherd calls to his scattered sheep, so there is a hand waving to us to press forward.

"We should be cloud climbers rather than mere mountain climbers. We should climb to see heights recede in continual folds of loveliness, and the clouds look their trailing purple shadows and sail slowly or hang motionless beyond the eternal buttresses.

"Is it because the wildwood passion of Pan still lingers in our hearts because still in our minds the voice of syrinx floats in melancholy music, the music of regret and longing that for most of us there is so potent a spell in running water? We associate them with loneliness and beauty, beauty and solitude...these are still the shepherd kings of the imagination—to compel our wandering memories, or thoughts, our dreams."

A yellowed newspaper clipping taped inside the book also indicates Gwen's thinking. Titled "Youth," and written by Samual Ullman, it clearly spoke to Gwen, who, despite her sharp tongue and critical eye, viewed life with the optimism of a spring bloom:

"Youth is not a time of life, it is a state of mind. It is not a matter of rosy cheeks, red lips and supple knees. It is a matter of the will. A quality of imagination, vigor of the emotions, it is the freshness of the deep springs of life.

"Youth means the temperamental predominance of courage over timidity, of the appetite for adventure over the love of ease. This often exists in a man of 60 more than a boy of 20. Nobody grows old merely by living a number of years, we grow old by deserting our ideals.

"Years may wrinkle the skin, but to give up enthusiasm wrinkles the soul. Worry, fear, self doubt bows the heart and turns the spirit back to dust. Whether 60 or 16, there is in every human being's heart the lure of wonder, the unfailing, childlike curiosity of what's next, and the joy of the game of living.

"In the center of your heart and mind, there is a wireless station. So long as it receives messages of beauty, hope, cheer and courage, you are young. When the aerials are down and your spirit is covered with snows of cynicism and the ice of pessimism, then you have grown old, even at 20. But so long as your aerials are up to catch the optimism, there is hope you may die young at 80."

Gwen's own prose reflected these book passages and the newspaper clipping.

"I think we should all have a tree we could look up to," she once said in a speech. "A tree that can be an inspiration in time of need. Pick out your own tree and relate to it. And every time you need a source of inspiration, it will be there for you to look at. A tree, maybe it got hit by lightning, and it goes on living. You know that you too can meet the storms of life and go on living, because your tree did.

"A tree each year, at the end of all the twigs, will form new buds. The limbs will grow a little longer and the tips of the branches will remain forever young. The same way with you. With each day, you reach a little further, each day you learn something new, the tops of your mind will remain forever young—no matter how many years you count on your birthday."

From *Ruminate:*

Imagination and fantasy —
keep life fresh and intriguing ...
Instead of viewing clouds as
omens of changing weather —
see those great white puffs
against the blue as sculptures
in the air — see random
designs in motion —
— and dream .....
Let imagination run free —
allow fantasy to soar ....
Where new ideas form
the realm of creativeness ...
Dream great dreams today !!

But just as one is seduced into thinking Gwen is sentimental or ethereal, she corrects that course. During her early writing days, she was equally inspired by the work of Ayn Rand, whose philosophies matched Gwen's dedication to cool self-sufficiency at any cost; she must have identified with Rand's intellectual arrogance. Gwen also loved the clean, functional, nature-embracing architecture of Frank Lloyd Wright.

Gwen spent much of her free time alone, walking the woods near the cottage or along the Frankfort shore, sketching, jotting down notes. Since she was never known to date, she spent her evenings, after various dinner engagements, alone.

But some time in the 1950s, Gwen took in a roommate—a local teacher. It was a replication of the single-teacher/rooming-house world of Fred Frostic, long vanished by the '60s. Gwen never had lost her parents' enthusiasm for education and educators. Now deceased, the teacher and Gwen appeared to be very good friends, going out to lunch and dinner often and sharing the apartment over the Frankfort shop. Little is known about this friendship, other than the teacher eventually moved out, possibly because the widowed Florence moved in.

As Gwen carved out her living and her legacy, her family prospered as well. Elder brother Kenneth married and had a daughter. He never completed college but did well in advertising. Helen and her husband, Neil Warren, lived well on Neil's architect's salary. Helen was a teacher, earned a master's degree, did freelance writing, and was president of the Michigan Division of the American Association of University Women. They had no children.

Andy became a dentist and had five children, including Bill, who has worked most of his life for Gwen. Don, a commercial painter and master gardener, had two children. Margaret, an educator with a master's degree, had three children. Ralph, a teacher and later a principal, had two children. He earned a master's degree and did at least some work on his doctorate.

All the Frostic children were civic minded, as their parents had taught and modeled. Some would at some point in their lives have an interest in special education or in helping people with disabilities. Helen, for example, worked with visually handicapped people, Margaret with the mentally disabled.

Sometimes one of Gwen's sisters or brothers and their families visited Gwen's shop, often staying at the cottage. Gwen always treated them well enough, but the odd Frostic bond ruled, especially with Gwen; it was there, but at arm's length. Helen said that she, Margaret and Andy were close, but Gwen seldom asked any of her siblings for help or for company. She did, in later years, vacation in the Upper Peninsula, Arizona and California with her brother Andy and his wife Edna. Gwen was not independently mobile enough to vacation alone, especially after the disappearance of the mass transit of the early 1900s. These were for the most part pleasant trips, Edna recalls. Occasionally she and Andy had to help Gwen get over rough terrain on hikes. When the trio visited the zoo in San Diego about 15 years ago, Gwen avoided tedious walking. She spent the day in the hummingbird house. Sometimes, Gwen spoke critically of family members to her employees or others—following her tradition with many other people. Gwen was quick to find fault and to articulate it.

But, as one of Gwen's Frankfort friends observed once, "there is no pattern to what Gwen does." Many years later, when Gwen's brother, Don, turned 75, Gwen called his wife and children and suggested throwing him a big birthday party.

"I about fell over," said Janet Cashin, Don's daughter, who lives in the Wyandotte area.

Gwen was particularly steadfast in family crises. In 1973, Helen's husband, Neil, had a thumb removed due to cancer. It was a difficult period for the couple, and Helen told Gwen about their joy when Neil learned to tie his own shoelaces again. Helen believes Gwen always rather liked Neil. He had spent a lot of time chatting with Gwen back when Gwen had her metal shop in the Frostic home shortly after Sara Frostic died. "They developed quite a relationship," Helen said. "There's a family legend that Gwen paid Neil to take me off her hands. And Gwen's never denied it."

Upon news of Neil's success with the shoelaces, Gwen wrote Helen an extraordinary letter revealing a seldom seen softer side—an instinctive empathy, her ability to derive joy and hope from nature under any circumstances, and a rare articulation of her own thoughts about her "handicap":

Dear Helen:

— A long time ago your mother and mine faced a difficult decision: whether in the name of love — to help — to shelter — to answer all the every day needs or to be seemingly unconcerned and unkind by not allowing sympathy and love to guide her ways. I am the result of that decision.

Today you face a similar decision. It takes courage to resist the desire to "help," when it's so much easier to do something rather than let Neil work out new ways to do — even so simple a thing as to tie his own shoelaces.

But you'll deny him the supreme joy of independence if you are not as strong a person as your mother. Let him try everything, even things he shouldn't do — now — not later. This is the greatest love you can give.

— Gwen

"I didn't know the strong feeling she had for Mama," Helen later said about the letter's contents. "I think she really felt a strong connection there, she really felt the intent of Mama to let Gwen do what she did."

One year later, in 1974, Helen was diagnosed with endometrial cancer. Gwen's first reaction was to say that Helen couldn't have cancer because no Frostic had ever had cancer. Margaret pointed out that radiation was (at the time) only used for cancer patients, but, Helen said, "that didn't change Gwen's mind."

Once again, Gwen sent her support in a heartfelt, handwritten letter:

Dear Helen —

I know that you and Neil always have wanted to share everything — but this is ridiculous — !

— Now comes the long period of treatment and recuperation — take it day at a time — it will be easier. It will seem long only if you look back — or try to look ahead. Each day by itself will be much the same as all your days, filled with little surprises — as a new bird arrives or the buds burst into flowers — and the hundreds of little things that have made your life interesting. It's a wonderful time of year to keep interested outside yourself — and you have a wonderful place to do just that.

Having gone through this type of thing with Neil has prepared you somewhat — it will give you assurance that the combination of medical science and time can produce miracles.

With all universal life — man can discover what is happening — and perhaps how it happens — but never why — don't try!

It's so nice to have had dinner at Andy's with you, just like old times. I enjoyed it a lot and all of the things you did especially for me.

There's a wooley bear crawling up the screen — the gold finches are turning yellow — and I still have shingles.

Love Gwen

Helen considered the letter memorable—and has kept it all these years—not just for the support but because it was the only time Helen knew of that Gwen used the word "love" in a letter—and probably among the few times she used it at all. It was also one of the few times Gwen acknowledged any health problems. She struggled with the shingles for some time.

Such tender moments with Gwen were limited. For the most part, Gwen was much of what her mother had been. If nothing else, she was remarkably consistent, never changing. Outwardly unemotional, direct, hardworking, unyielding, she kept her life and surroundings simple, reflecting the modest, make-do world of her childhood, yet she seldom dwelled in the past. She did not buy superfluous things—other than roomy Cadillacs—and did not replace a working or useful item, no matter how old; when she had her hair cut at a local salon, she did not stay to have it dried. She wore simple, tasteful and tailored clothes. She never built a big estate to replace her little apartment; what for? She always financed her own business expansions and never did anything until she could afford it. And when she could afford an expansion, it was well-executed and worthwhile.

In the early 1960s, Gwen learned that a marina was planned for the swamp in downtown Frankfort. It was widely believed that she was deeply upset about this marina. Even her good friends describe her almost personal relationship with the wetland. She spent hours there sketching. "She knew every bird and turtle in that marsh," said Mollie Rogers, Gwen's long-time friend. Local editor John Peterson said Gwen made known her objection to the marina and that the town's response was that "it was better for us as a marina than to entertain birds."

Gwen was too practical, too business minded, to object to the marina. She had no feelings about it, she said later. The entire Frankfort area was still vastly rural, a wonderland of forests, lakes and beaches. The birds would come anyway, she knew. Besides, by then, she had her eye on another swamp area seven miles south of Frankfort in Benzonia. A 40-acre piece of property along the Betsie River, full of trees, wildlife and fields, was for sale. Gwen decided she would build her own shop there.

She found the woman who owned the property. The woman wondered why Gwen was so interested in the property. It was just a swamp. But Gwen's interest made her suspicious.

"When I first went to buy this land, I asked the woman, 'What do you want for it?' But it was ideal for an artist so I persisted. She backed out of the deal three times because she started thinking that there must be a pot of gold under some tree. I told her she should stop looking for it because she'd never find it."

The deal done, Gwen talked to builder Jim Rogers, Mollie's husband, who looked at the property dubiously, as did others. Why would Gwen want to relocate an increasingly successful business right on the main street of a tourist town out here—in the middle of nowhere?

Gwen and Mollie took long walks all over, while Gwen's trained eye took in the diversity and beauty of raw nature. She saw what no others did—a paradise and a chance to finally own her own place, her own future. According to her vision, people would actually make a special trip to drive to this scruffy swampland to buy stationery. Her business colleagues just shook their heads.

In the early 1960s, Gwen broke ground for what is arguably the most unusual construction project in Michigan. She had no actual plans and never considered an architect. She and Rogers just talked.

She wanted a balcony overlooking the pressroom and an office facing the pond, she said. She wanted the footings in by September 1, floor by October 1, roof by November 1. She wanted to open April 26, 1964, although she did not know what day of the week April 26th—her birthday—fell on.

"What time?" Rogers asked Gwen.

"Ten o'clock," Gwen said.

Gwen and Rogers went out the property and set out four stakes. A neighbor dropped by. "You should make it bigger," the neighbor said. They did. From then on, it was like Margaret's former adventures with Gwen in the kitchen. Gwen later said of her building, "I didn't design it, we just grew it."

"Can you get any big stones?" she asked Rogers

"Yeah, all the farms around here have big rock piles," Rogers replied.

"Good. Get some. Get a lot of them."

Rogers went to a farmer, who offered to cut the huge boulders. "Well, no," Rogers said, "she wants them big."

The stones were hauled to the building site. Gwen told Rogers' crew she did not want the rocks piled up in any certain way. "I want them to look like they fell there," she said. "Make 'em look comfortable and put some cement around them."

The men, feeling their way, went back and forth between Benzonia and Gwen's Frankfort shop. They hauled her back out to Frankfort after they erected the first couple of boulders.

Gwen nodded her approval. "Go ahead," she encouraged them, "just think free. Put 'em up. Don't look for any special stone. Every stone is beautiful."

The rocks came for months and formed the retaining walls, fireplace and later the center of a round house addition to the shop.

When crews hit a natural flowing well, Gwen said to turn it into a fountain inside the shop. When the beams were going up, Gwen said to space them irregularly. When the roundhouse was added, Gwen said to make the roof sod. When crews finished pouring the cement floor nice and smooth, Gwen told Rogers to cut off the feet of road kill and put their footprints in the wet cement. She wanted plant imprints, too.

Rogers relayed the instruction to his dubious crew. "Now you have to pick ferns and leaves and lay them on the cement and pick them up later."

The crew leader shook his head. "I spent all day getting this perfect."

Orders were orders. The men traipsed out into the woods and looked for ferns, feeling a little stupid. They brought them back, laid them into the cement, still feeling stupid. Then they lifted them up—and saw the effect. Before long, the men were like children with clay.

And so it went. Sliced tree trunks became benches, wall covering was sliced logs—bark side up—and branches were hand rails. Driftwood became doorknobs, branches stretched across stumps and logs made fences. Walkways outdoors were mulch. There was no suggestion of "landscaping." Nature was landscaping, let her do what she wants.

"Whatever will grow, I'll let it," she once said. "I haven't any right to cut it. I don't have the right to decide what will grow and what will not. In the end, everything is beneficial to something else. Of course, if a mosquito was biting me, I'd kill it."

The shop design purposely concealed any view of Gwen's second floor apartment, which was as unique as the rest of the shop. Her back wall overlooking the pond was all glass. There were two large screened in porches for major league bird feeding, where Gwen began to put out buckets of birdseed. There were no doors in the apartment, no curtains, no walls, only "divisions," as she called them. "Walls would break up the flow. And I don't like lamps. I have lighted panels." There were a few small adjacent rooms for Florence, who lived with Gwen for 10 years until two years before her 1994 death.

Downstairs, the shop had two levels. Shoppers on the upper level had an unobstructed view of the lower level, where Gwen's four Heidelberg presses kept the rhythm of a fast-expanding business. A smaller room in the back was Gwen's growing nature library.

When the shop was ready to open, Gwen sent out announcements: "We have moved to the frog pond, Teddy and I," read one. "Come wonder and wander with us," read another.

The new shop opened for business April 26, 1964. It was Gwen's 58th birthday. Fifty years after she had romped around a wild Grosse Ile and 70 years since her father had discovered the beauty of Michigan in a field fossil, Gwen Frostic had her own piece of nature and a business plan no one could understand.

Gwen hoped for maybe a couple of hundred people at her Grand Opening. About 1,000 came, prompting Gwen to observe about the event years later that there weren't nearly enough cookies.

Dreams Without Work are Fantasy, Work Without Dreams is Drudgery

The wildflowers, weeds and trees grew slowly around Presscraft Papers in Benzonia in the years after the new shop opened. The customers multiplied quickly. Eventually, they came not only from Michigan but from all 50 states and, over time, from dozens of foreign countries. Presscraft Papers became a required tourist stop in the Traverse City and Frankfort areas.

Gwen's press room gradually filled up with Heidelberg presses—15 in all by the 1980s. She printed thousands of her books and stationery packages and she added new products, such as place mats. She turned her first million and began hiring more employees, especially in the summer months. Her phenomenal success brought invitations to speak all over Michigan, which in turn encouraged media interviews. By the 1970s, Gwen's work and her wisdom had become a fixture in Michigan and by the 1980s, she was a bona fide state institution. This period, between about 1970 and 1987, was Gwen's golden age.

During these years, she made up to 40 speaking trips a year, packing her trunk with products and taking off in her Cadillac to all kinds of places: the town hall in Adrian, a small college in Grosse Pointe, a junior high school in Romeo, a women's seminar in Three Rivers, another at Michigan State University, the Owosso Country Club, the Northville Historical Society, the Genessee Area Skills Center and dozens more.

She spoke in her little hometown of Croswell when she donated money for the church addition named in honor of her Uncle Lou. She also went to St. Charles, where she so long before had lived with her family and their horse and carriage. Her appearance helped raise funds for the Hartley Outdoor Education Center. Robert Loomis, chairman and CEO of Community State Bank in St. Charles, recalled Gwen whirled into town for a meal and speech, and then right back out of town. In her speech, Gwen talked about the beauty of the Bad River and childhood memories.

Gwen never accepted a fee for these appearances and she always paid her own expenses. Her speeches were primarily inspirational, with titles such as "Strengthening Respect for Women's Capabilities."

"We make napkins and books and notepaper," she told one group, "but this is not our aim. Our aim is to bring you the wind and the trees and the very first violet of spring. Our aim is to bring you a bit of serenity that exists in this world, serenity that you must not forget, in spite of the headlines in the paper...."

Gwen offered philosophical advice of her own variety. The woman in this more public venue was balanced, happy with who she was, wise and, at times, humorous. Some of her advice: "Be part of your own drama... Do your own thinking.... Dreams without work are fantasy, work without dreams is drudgery.... There's never a problem you will face that you cannot solve yourself.... You will never get an idea about something you know nothing about.... There's always more than one way to do something. Seek the alternative.... Progress doesn't need to be destruction."

"Nothing is ever absolute," she told one audience. "Two times two not only makes four. Put them next to each other, they make 22. 'You have two ice cubes and they melt, what do you have?' a little boy was once asked," Gwen said. "And the little boy said: Spring time."

Creativity is freedom, knowledge is creativity, Gwen said in 1985 during a public television show and the only video program about her known to exist. When asked if art and business are a "natural combination," Gwen answered, "I don't think they were put together, I don't think they were ever separated."

One of Gwen's favorite stories was about a man she met walking through the woods behind her shop. "I was coming up from the river down there and he didn't know who I was, which was perfectly all right. And he said to me, 'Is there anything farther on?' And I said, 'Well, have you seen anything yet? Because if you haven't seen anything yet, there's nothing farther on.' And that's true no matter what it is. You will have to see in order to become....'"

"Fill yourselves full," Gwen urged a group of art students in the early 1970s. "Do all the reading that you can. Study all the math and science that you can. Don't take anything whole from a book. In order to be real, you must be yourself."

"I have always had time to do what I want," she told another group. "I am doing everything I hoped to do, but that doesn't mean I have ceased to grow. I am always evolving."

Gwen often told stories about her customers. "We just finished printing 200,000 of the gray and white chickadee papers," she told a 1960s interviewer. "It's the most popular. But a woman sent hers back with a note saying, 'I am returning the things you call chickadees. Neither I nor my friends recognize them.' I wrote back: 'I am returning your money, plus postage, plus the nickel for the stamp on your letter. If you ever sat in the woods and watched the little fellows, you'd recognize them.'

"Later the woman wrote again. I'm returning half the money. I've decided they're not half so bad.

"Another customer wrote, 'I am returning your book because there are blank pages in it.' I wrote back, 'I'm returning your money—I meant them to be blank.'"

Gwen told the following story to the *P.E.O. Record* in 1971. It especially captures her unique sense of humor.

"In our book *Wing Borne,* we have a little duck that came around to the studio and said he wanted to get in the book. I was all done with the book, and I said, 'You'll have to wait until the next one.' There was an argument and finally he got in, but his head sticks out one place and about five pages later, there's his tail. He got in between the sections, you see. We knew we'd get letters about this. One came from a bookseller in California. 'I'm returning 30 books,' she said. 'They are all misbound.' I wrote to her and told her I was giving her credit for the 30 books, that they were not misbound, but that the little duck just wanted to be there and there wasn't anything I could do about it.

"She wrote back and thanked me and said she wanted 50 books with the duck in the right place because California taste must be quite different than Michigan taste. So I wrote to her: 'I have had a conference with the duck, and he refuses to bow to California.'"

Gwen loved these speaking trips—they were like vacations—and those who accompanied her did as well. Her drivers would vary. Sometimes her nephew Bill drove, sometimes Evelyn Argue. The cleaning lady-turned-driver thoroughly enjoyed her boss's more relaxed and entertaining frame of mind. Florence often served as Gwen's chauffeur during the time the two lived together. Gwen's feelings for Florence were never any more clear than those she had for anyone else, but she did mention Florence in a speech or two:

"I have a stepmother who is 87," Gwen said in a speech in the mid-1980s, "who is very successful in her life... But she has no sense of humor, and it's awful." A sense of humor was essential, Gwen tried to tell Florence, "but Florence said, I can't find anything funny to laugh at. I said, 'Florence, you don't find funny things, they're all around you. Look in the mirror when you get up in the morning.' Of course, she didn't think that was funny...."

During many of her newspaper interviews, Gwen weighed in on the issues of the day. She was part-conservative, part-bootstraps, all Gwen. She also displayed a kind of classism typical of the early 1900s:

"We try to make everyone the same today," she said in a 1970s interview, "but that's not nature's way. Why take people in poverty brackets and compare them to us? We don't understand their needs. In nature, there are different types of birds with no desire to dominate each other. Man is as different from man as bird from bird."

"When they decided they should educate everybody, they began to have trouble," she said in another interview. "They spend all their time and money on people who can't be educated and let people like you and me go by the wayside. All men are not created equal. You aren't equal with people who dropped out of high school, I hope. We need to put more of an emphasis on people with ability. There will always be the rich and the poor."

Gwen told a business and professional women's group that "in any movement, you have the mainstream and the fringe people. The mainstream goes down the center and the fringe people get the publicity. In the women's movement, you had women burning brassieres and others who wanted to join men's clubs. What they needed was just to sit down, work something out and get it off the front pages. I never felt discrimination. I think discrimination is in the mind of the person discriminated against. I sat in this seat so I wouldn't have to worry about it. In other words, I'm the one in control.

"Women have gained all the things they stood for. They don't need the law to tell them they're equal. They are equal."

As early as the 1960s, Gwen began to receive significant recognition in Michigan. In 1965, she received a Doctor of Fine Arts Degree from Albion College and Doctor of Laws from Eastern Michigan University. She received a Doctor of Humanities Degree from Western Michigan University in 1971. On that occasion, WMU President Dr. James Miller said that Gwen Frostic "is what all colleges hope their students achieve in their lifetime." Michigan State University awarded Gwen a Doctorate of Fine Arts in 1973 and Alma College a Doctorate of Literature in 1977.

Gwen never called herself an environmentalist, and those most active in the movement wouldn't either. But her work during the early and fervent days of the movement, observers believed, advanced the environmental cause simply by showcasing it so well. As a result, Gwen was given awards or honorary memberships by the Michigan Botanical Club, Federated Garden Clubs of Michigan, the Michigan Audubon Society, and the National Wildlife Federation. She was awarded the Sarah Chapman Francis Literary Award by the Garden Clubs of America in 1972.

In 1970, Gwen's middle-of-nowhere business, by then the solid tourist destination she had envisioned, was recognized when the Michigan Tourist Association bestowed upon Gwen its Distinguished Service Award.

Two of the more significant awards came nearly 10 years apart. In 1978, Michigan Governor Bill Milliken proclaimed

May 23 as Gwen Frostic Day in Michigan. In 1986, two years after the Michigan Women's Hall of Fame was established by the Michigan Women's Studies Association, Gwen received the Hall's Life Achievement Award for "distinction in the field of arts and letters, business and industry, religion and philosophy." Gwen, according to one nominating letter, overcame "significant physical handicaps," to produce her art and poetry and that "her work reflects her deep love and understanding of life around her.... She is a gentle and caring person whose writings and drawings show how much she cares for the beauty of the outdoors in Michigan and how she shares this feeling with others."

The panel in the Hall of Fame, located in Lansing, does not mention Gwen's "handicap," which Gwen likely appreciated. Gwen was inducted into the Hall of Fame with Helen Thomas, White House Bureau Chief for United Press International, Reverend Marjorie Swan Matthews, the first female Bishop of the United Methodist Church, Dr. Marjorie Peebles-Meyers, the first black woman to graduate from Wayne State University's medical school, Mary Chase Perry Stratton, founder of Pewabic Pottery in Detroit, Elmina R. Lucke, founder of the International Institute in Detroit and Elizabeth C. Crosby, the first woman to hold a full professorship at the University of Michigan Medical School.

Recognition and wealth had no apparent effect on Gwen. Her life, her work, continued. Every day, she walked her property with her sketch pad and her dog, just as she always had. Most every night, she carved at her table in her apartment. She worked all day and greeted customers. She wore her hair short and wore simple work dresses as she always had. She wrote one book, then another and another, setting the type of every word of every book by hand, alone. For a while, mainly due to Florence's interest, Gwen had a shop in Arizona, which she occasionally visited.

Her circle of friends and admirers widened and included such distinguished people as Diether Haenicke, then president of Western Michigan University, a beneficiary of an unspecified but substantial donation from Gwen. Haenicke remarked that Gwen, among other things, was "a good judge of horse flesh." When he visited her once with another member of the WMU staff, Gwen made her dislike of the gentleman quite clear. Haenicke didn't blame her—he didn't like the man either.

Gwen, partly out of self-interest and partly out of more charitable concerns, helped Benzie County businesses to compete with the far more visible and vibrant Traverse City area. She bought one building in Benzonia so that the Benzie County Chamber of Commerce could use it virtually rent-free. Her only stipulation was that one room in the building had to be open for the free use of small groups who could not afford other accommodations. Years later, the thriving chamber bought the building from Gwen for a very reasonable price. Gwen quietly helped other businesses get started.

She also offered her unsolicited opinion. About 20 years ago, Kirk and Pam Lorenz bought a local restaurant that they eventually turned into an upscale restaurant and hotel called the Brookside Inn. The day they opened, Gwen strolled into the place and looked Kirk Lorenz over.

"So, you're the new owners," she announced.

Gwen sat down and had lunch. She picked up the paper place mat that featured the Michigan Fruit Growers Association. "You shouldn't have this," she said.

"I said, 'Okaaaay,'" Kirk Lorenz recalled. "That was about noon. By 5:00 P.M., in comes Bill with thousands of place mats designed by Gwen. We've used them ever since."

As the years passed, so did some of Gwen's family and friends. Kenneth, her oldest brother, was killed in an auto accident in 1957. Andy died in the early 1990s. Ralph died in the late 1980s. After living with Gwen for 10 years, Florence died in the early 1990s in Ann Arbor. Family members rarely heard from Gwen casually, but always for birthdays or other major family events and in those family crises. She would send money unexpectedly as well.

Gwen, the sick child doctors said wouldn't live long, headed into her 70s and then her 80s with relatively few ailments. She suffered the bout with shingles once and had eye surgery. Walking became more difficult, the limp more pronounced, her speech more slurred, but she was quite unchanged for the most part.

One day during the 1980s—the date is not certain—Gwen fell down her stairs and broke both of her wrists. Her physician predicted she would never be able to use her hands again. That was all Gwen needed to hear—she was carving linoleum in no time.

The Circularity of It All

In the late 1990s, nearly 35 years after the triumphant opening of Gwen's Benzonia shop, the place is slowly melting back into its natural surroundings. No lawn mowers, no rakes, no string trimmers have ever touched the grounds. It is easy to imagine that in a few more decades a stranger could come upon the area and discern no building at all. This is quite obviously Gwen's plan—to have a shop living and dying at the same time, perhaps imitating a part of nature she calls "the circularity of it all." Trees have grown tall on the sod roof. Evergreens, saplings and natural grasses rise high around the walls of Presscraft Papers. Vines curl helter-skelter, trees lean, and leaves carpet the mulch walkways.

Gwen presently owns 285 wild acres around her shop. It takes only a walk behind the shop to remember just how loud a forest can be. Birds chirp, twitter and caw unremittingly. Trees swish, ducks splash-land into the pond, leaves rustle mysteriously. You sense a multitude of small animals gossiping about you. Gwen's property has become as lovely, with nature as its true owner, as her linoleum images.

Inside, the shop is comfortably what it was the day Gwen opened. The doorknob is the same piece of driftwood. The flowing well fountain still bubbles just inside the door. To the left stands the graceful fire dragon fire screen Gwen made about 70 years ago. Nearby is the copper sundial she made, equally aged.

The rest of Presscraft Papers is visible at a glance, thanks to Gwen's open design. It has the clean lines of a museum. Gwen's products sit on plain wood shelves and panels along the length of the shop and in small antechambers. Framed pictures, wrapping paper, coffee cups, tote bags and Gwen's books are among the products added since 1964.

The cardinal is still there, perched on note cards and inside nice frames. Also present are the blue jay and raccoon, long time favorites. The packages of calendars, place mats, note paper, and postcards still sit wrapped simply in plastic—no exclamation points, no slogans, no advertisements. The animal and plant floor imprints done by those cement workers so long ago are intact. Sometimes Gwen tells customers animals sneaked inside the building before the cement dried. Sometimes, the customers believe her.

Tucked behind the office area is Gwen's renowned nature library. One photograph of Fred and another of Sara hangs on the wall, Fred's face oblong and kind, Sara with a harder gleam in her eye. Beneath Papa and Mama is a row of oval framed photos of Gwen, Kenneth, Helen, Ralph and Bill as very small children.

But the words "nature library" belie the contents of the small room, which has two windowed walls facing

Gwen's forest. Many of the books in the library are historic and valuable—and part of Fred's living legacy in Gwen's life. Many of the books were collected and signed by Fred in fading fountain pen script. It was almost as if Fred were sitting in the room. Books, many of them fragile and leather bound, that were his or signed by him include: *Home Studies in Nature,* 1885; *Plant Relations—A First Book of Botany,* 1905; *A Handbook of Flowering Plants and Ferns of the Central and Northeastern United States and Adjacent Canada,* 1908; *Old Time School and School Books,* 1908; *The Childhood of Animals,* 1912; *The Plants of Michigan,* 1918; *Animals of the Past,* 1922; *Around the World With Kipling,* 1926 which bears the pre-Nazi inside cover design of a swastika.

Some of the plants in these aged books have probably themselves disappeared. Other unusual volumes include a very small, very old copy of Thoreau's *Walden—A Life in the Woods,* possibly an early edition. There is also an undated book of poems by William Cullen Bryant.

Another small book has a handwritten identification inside: "Hardbound, September, 1928, by S. Gwendolen Frostic, Western State Teachers' College, Kalamazoo."

About Ourselves: Psychology for Normal People, 1927, was one of Gwen's early college texts. A 1923 type style book is presumably among her first printer's books, but may have belonged to her father.

Many of the remaining book titles resemble the kind of lyrical, whimsical language Gwen used to describe nature: *The Geese Fly High, Falling Leaves, The Way of the Wil-*

derness, *The Uncommon Loon, The Dog Observed, Hens Teeth and Horses Toes.*

But it is still Gwen that people really come to see. The sight of her sitting at her desk, as she has for so long, is an indescribable comfort to Michiganders.

One day in the summer of 1998 featured a typical, familiar scene. People lined up at the counter while clerks wrapped their orders in Gwen's wrapping paper and taped to them a small evergreen sprig. Others mulled all around the shop, and, sooner or later, tiptoed through the half-door leading to the office area, where sat the diminutive figure of the artist-in-residence. Visible through the window behind her was the O'Hare International of all duck ponds. Dozens of birds landed, took off and taxied on the old frog pond. Next to her was her wheelchair and next to her wheelchair, lying like a bear rug, was Eliot, Gwen's retriever. She was named after 19th century novelist George Eliot, who was really Marion Evans using a pseudonym, but that wasn't why Gwen called the female dog "him." She did so because, she told everyone, "all dogs are he and all cats are she." Gwen tossed dog biscuits, Vanilla wafers and ice cubes to the aged dog.

Gwen was the same, yet not the same—incredibly old— 92—her face wrinkled and her head leaning very noticeably to one side. But from that face stared two sharp eyes—hawk's eyes. Anyone who might have thought Gwen was losing leaves needed only to talk to her. Many did, making the pilgrimage up to her as if she were as holy and amiable as Mother Teresa. One woman from North Carolina got Gwen's autograph on a framed block print. Gwen used her brown ink signing pen, making her trademark G and F, her rigid thumb gripping the pen hard. Next came an older woman from Dayton, Ohio.

"You have a busy place here, Gwen. Looks like you're doin' well, are you Gwen? You keep up the good cheer! We'll see you another year!"

A woman in her 20s breathed, "I love your pictures! They're so beautiful." A family with three children posed for a picture with Gwen. They were from Pennsylvania.

"We order your things all the time," the mother said.

"Thank you," Gwen said.

"I like your dog. What's his name?"

"I don't know. He never writes it."

The woman chuckled. "Are you still working every day?"

"What else would I do for fun?"

The woman laughed.

A man suddenly came up with his little girl, looking urgent. "Can we use the rest room?" the man asked.

"No," Gwen said.

Appalled, the man rushed off. "We had a public rest room," Gwen explained, "but the people didn't know how to use it. One woman raised a bunch of Cain about not having a rest room and not getting waited on. People should boycott me, she said. She raised so much Cain. But she bought $30 worth."

The line went on, all afternoon. A Florida man came up. Eliot barked. "He barks at all men," Gwen said.

One of two men told Gwen, "My friend finally made it."

"Where you been all your life?" Gwen said.

"Is that your dog?"

"I'm his. There's a lot of difference."

"We come every year," a couple said. Gwen asked where they lived.

"We're from Michigan, but we moved to Ohio," the woman replied.

"Shame on you."

When a man said he owned a shop in Suttons Bay, Gwen immediately asked, "How's business?" When someone asked what her favorite product was, she said, "I don't have a favorite anything. I think if you have a favorite, it cuts you off from other things."

A tender moment suddenly occurred when a young boy came in with his father and brothers. Gwen's face brightened unexpectedly—uncharacteristically—and she motioned the little boy close. He came up to her chair and, in a gesture few of her close friends would believe, hugged the child. Perhaps it was the memory of her little brothers—of Bill and Ralph, by then long gone.

But Gwen soon was back to normal, greeting customers fairly steadily the rest of the day. It was a remarkable performance. She was never caught speechless. When people asked if they could write a check, she replied, "How should I know if you can write a check?" When someone asked her age, she said, "Well, I don't buy green bananas anymore."

But there was a sense, and still is, that nature will soon claim Gwen. In early 1999, Gwen took ill and was not at her desk for a few weeks. About a year earlier, she had had an infection that weakened her so much that she finally consented to hire a personal assistant. Not long before that, she also submitted to a leg brace and then, finally, the wheelchair.

Her dinners out have diminished greatly, though she still goes out for lunch. Her evenings remain much the same: she carves, she watches a few television shows, such as "Murder She Wrote," "Jeopardy," "Wheel of Fortune," "Dr. Quinn, Medicine Woman," and the Dallas Cowboys, "because they know how to win," she once said. She watches church services Sunday mornings and reads books usually related to nature or science but two favorites include *When I Get Old I Shall Wear Purple,* and *If I had My Life to Live Over Again.*

Gwen still takes drives—steering her drivers on every back road, she knows them all by heart. But she has switched from her favored Cadillacs to Lincolns "because you can't tell a Cadillac from a Chevrolet anymore."

Twice a day, Gwen still feeds the creatures from her side porch, or has her nephew Bill do it—reminiscent of the 150 feeding geese she entertained in her tiny Frankfort yard 40 years ago. She goes through a 33-gallon-bag of peanuts and uncounted pounds of birdseed each week. Like a Disney film, Gwen has all kinds of regular creature acquaintances—a woodpecker, a squirrel, and the ducks that fall upon the pond at feeding time. Gwen knows their habits, she knows that most animals feed in daylight and that come dusk, they, like people, go to sleep. Gwen often refers to her daily bird feeding, when birds swarm the feeders on her screen porches, as "cheaper than going to the opera."

Gwen spends holidays alone, perfectly happy, or perhaps dining with her good friends, Pam and Kirk Lorenz at the Brookside. The couple sees much of Gwen. They discuss politics, business and local gossip. There is no dredging of the past with Gwen.

Gwen, Kirk Lorenz said, "is the smartest person I've ever run into—still is. I've talked to a lot of people, college professors and presidents and right on down the line. Get into a conversation with Gwen, it's a conversation."

Pam is Gwen's current best friend, although when asked, Gwen would not deem her such. But she has expressed her affection for Pam by giving her one of her original printing plates, along with other gifts. Gwen especially likes to give people prisms, reminiscent of that in her mother's dining room so long ago.

In early 1998, Gwen was working on her new book, which involved Bible passages—a choice that reinforced the observation that Gwen follows no pattern. Pam was over one evening and flipped through the tissue-thin pages of the old Frostic Bible, decorated by Fred's fading script recording the births of Frostic children nearly 100 years ago. Gwen had told Pam that the only picture she had ever had of her mother had been stolen from her shop many years before. But Pam found tucked into the Bible pages a photograph of a woman with soft, curly hair and a hard gleam in her eye. Scrawled on the backside of the picture was "Sara Frostic."

Excited, Gwen leaned over and stared at the picture—Mama. Thus, Sara took her rightful place next to Fred in Gwen's nature library.

Afterword

The world that Sara and Fred knew, the world that hosted Gwen's birth at the beginning of a new century is gone—the horses, the saloons, the one room school houses, the muddy roads, the street cars, the open spaces on Grosse Ile, the modesty and make-do quality of life. One day, Gwen too, will be gone. It is nature's way.

What she will leave behind is not her concern, she has said many times. But it is Michigan's fortune. Gwen Frostic's legacy will be more than just an extraordinary business and unique, enduring art that will help preserve the memory of Michigan's natural beauty. It also illustrates what can happen when you work hard, imagine even harder, and think for yourself—even when others doubt your ability to do so, perhaps especially then: Gwen Frostic was always handicapped, Gwen Frostic was never handicapped—the circularity of it all.

No one knows what will happen to Presscraft Papers when Gwen is gone, though there are many rumors. Gwen won't say. But she has said once what she would like on her epitaph. It is from a famous poem written by English author Jan Struther: Here lies one doubly blest...She was happy...She knew it."

What Gwen does not want left behind is this or any other biography—much ado about nothing, she says. Besides, she has already written her biography, which she says was quite sufficient, along with her books. It goes like this:

She was born
of that there's no dispute
She goes to bed each night
and rises every morning
(tho not so very early)
eats breakfast — lunch and
dinner — and sometimes
in between...
She always liked to play with
blocks — the things boys did
seemed best of all — she liked
to hammer and to saw
She started school at six —
went thru all the grades and
college before she tackled
business....
— she wishes there were
more to tell
but that's the story
in a shell....

— Gwen Frostic